Papier Mâché

By the *Sunset* Editorial Staff with William J. Shelley and Barbara Linse

Lane Books • Menlo Park, California

ACKNOWLEDGMENTS

In order to create a craft book with interest for both adult and child, expert and novice, Sunset brought together several consultants who worked closely with the editors to offer a broad range of projects. Barbara Linse and William J. Shelley, papier mâché experts and teachers, contributed project ideas, designs, and photographs as well as background material. Mrs. Linse, assistant professor of education at San Francisco State College, contributed many ideas and worked with Sunset's editors in shaping up the original concept of the book. Mr. Shelley, an artist in his own right as well as an art teacher, lecturer, and supervisor of art education for the San Jose Unified School District, designed and photographed nearly all of the papier mâché projects presented here.

We would like to thank the many students and friends of our two consultants for their contributions. Their names appear next to the projects which they designed. A special thanks is due Kathleen Casey and Suki Graef for their work with Sunset Magazine and to Cynthia Clark for making several projects especially for this book.

Edited by Carol G. Blitzer
Illustrations: Susan S. Lampton
Layout and Graphics: Lawrence A. Laukhuf

Contents

Individual Projects

Papier Mâché objects from many countries show range of possibilities.

Introducing Papier Mâché

Many people associate the great versatility and varied functions of paper with the twentieth century, but paper construction is a craft dating back more than a thousand years. Soon after the Chinese invented paper, they began to experiment with ways of tearing it in pieces, mixing it with glue, and shaping or molding it into beautiful functional boxes, trays, and other pieces. No one knows the reason, but interest in this craft declined for several hundred years, and wasn't revived until the eighteenth century in France. It was there that the term papier mâché—literally, "chewed-up paper"—came to mean paper that was either torn in strips and glued, laminated in sheets, or broken down into a pulpy, claylike substance. The French became so interested in the versatility of this craft that soon it became part of the household scene—trays, snuff boxes, all sorts of containers, door panels, coach interiors, and some furniture pieces were made of papier mâché. There is even a record of papier mâché being used to build a ten-room house along with ten small cottages in the mid-nineteenth century. As a substitute for plaster in the molded ornaments of roofs and walls, it was sometimes called *carton pierre,* meaning "cardboard stone."

In more recent times, Japan, Mexico, India, and Portugal have begun to produce large quantities of papier mâché articles for export. These exports, including toy banks, vases, and decorative furniture pieces, characterize the wide range of projects possible. The photos below illustrate papier mâché crafts from around the world. For further instructions on methods for making papier mâché, turn to page 8.

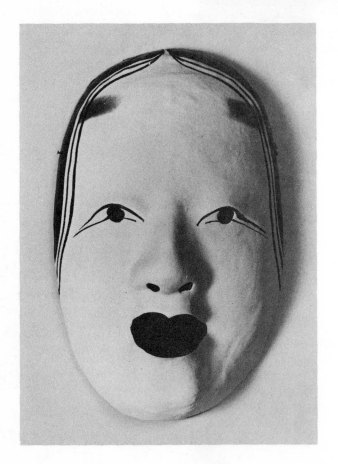

Examples from around the world: Opposite page, a Japanese mask, an elephant and rider from India, and Judas figures from Mexico; this page, an Italian scribe's box (made around 1740), another Japanese mask, and studio props from Hollywood.

Methods and Materials

There are three basic methods for making papier mâché. The most common is to dip strips of paper in a liquid adhesive and press them onto a base. You can use a ready-made base, such as a foil pan, a balloon, or a piece of fruit, or you can build your own base with anything from crumpled paper to chicken wire.

Another method is called lamination. It consists of gluing several layers of paper together to make one strong, flexible sheet. When laminated paper is wet, it can be shaped or molded over a base (or shaped by itself), or it can be torn into strips and applied to a base.

The third method is working with paper mash. Made of paper that is broken down into a claylike pulp, paper mash is often used to add texture and strength, but can also be molded like clay.

BASIC MATERIALS

Very simple materials are used in creating papier mâché objects. You'll need some kind of paper, paste, possibly a base to support the papier mâché, and paint or other decorative material (see pages 76-77). Often, most of the materials you'll need can be found around the house.

Kinds of paper. For most papier mâché projects you can use *any* kind of paper —newspaper, paper towels, white tissue paper, or facial tissue. You can often substitute an old bed sheet for part of the paper to give added strength. Cardboard egg cartons can be soaked and turned into paper mash.

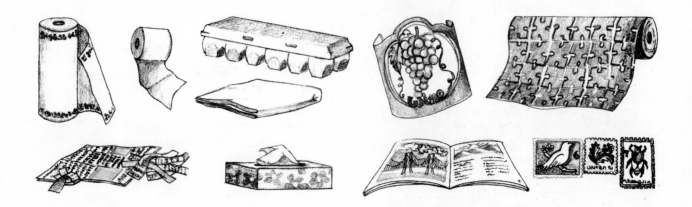

Many other kinds of papers can be used for adding decorative touches. You can use gift wrapping paper, cancelled postage stamps, note paper, colored tissue, playing cards, or magazine pictures. For specialty or boutique pieces, you can use labels from wine bottles and cosmetic jars and bottles. Wallpaper with distinct shapes and patterns can be used to make the overall design. Wallpaper sample books with discontinued patterns are often yours for the asking in paint, department, and furniture stores.

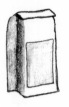

Paste and glue. Many different kinds of pastes and glues can be used for making papier mâché. The type of paste you use depends mostly on personal preference. In general, you should use stronger adhesives, such as wheat paste or diluted white glue, for making larger or more complex pieces.

One easy-to-use and efficient paste substitute is bottled liquid starch. For added strength, mix 2 tablespoons of salt, sand, or plaster with each quart of liquid starch.

You can also use non-toxic wallpaper paste to make a strong wheat paste. Slowly add 1 part of the paste to 10 parts of water. Mix thoroughly. If the solution becomes lumpy, strain it through cheesecloth or an old nylon stocking. You can add water if necessary to make the solution thin, but creamy. Keep the paste refrigerated. If not refrigerated, add oil of cloves or wintergreen (2 or 3 drops) as a preservative.

Another paste mixture often used to make papier mâché is made of 1 part liquid white glue and 1 part water.

Flour sauce glue is made by heating flour and water in a saucepan over a low flame. Continue adding water and stir until you have a creamy liquid. Chill and keep refrigerated. If not refrigerated, add oil of cloves or wintergreen.

Other glues, such as full strength white glue or rubber cement, can be used for adding final decorative touches.

Paper mash. Paper mash, or pulp, is made by soaking or cooking paper in water and combining with liquid adhesive to form a malleable substance. It can be molded over a base or by itself, and used to add texture or to build up specific areas.

There are several commercial mixes available for making "instant" paper mash. These mixtures are easy to work with and readily available at hobby or craft stores.

For more detailed directions on making paper mash, see page 66.

HOW TO DRY PAPIER MÂCHÉ

Adhesives should be applied sparingly to insure quick and even drying. You need only enough liquid to make paper strips or sheets stick together, or to thoroughly moisten paper mash and make it pliable. Any excess will retard the drying process.

After application of paper strips, laminated sheets, or paper mash, the project should be set aside to dry. Place the piece on a sheet of waxed paper (to avoid sticking), occasionally changing its position to insure even drying. Check the entire surface for dampness before proceeding to the next step.

If the surface isn't dry after 48 hours, place the project in bright sunlight or in a 175° oven with the door slightly open until thoroughly dry.

How to prevent warping. Papier mâché objects made without armatures may curl, bend, or even cave in a little during the drying process. Flat surfaces can be weighted down with rocks, books, or wood blocks covered with waxed paper. If the piece starts to sag while drying, use a sponge to moisten the surface, smooth it back into shape, and then apply a weight if necessary.

Applying Paper Strips to a Base

One of the easiest and most common ways of making papier mâché objects is to apply glued strips of newspapers, paper towels, craft paper—whatever paper you have on hand—to a base. Strips that have been torn rather than cut have a rough edge and will mesh together for a smoother surface. The paper may be torn into any size or shape depending on the particular piece of work—long strips may be used for large pieces with straight lines, shorter strips for smaller or round objects.

By tearing the paper against a ruler, you can make relatively uniform strips and make your work proceed more rapidly. You can also tear several layers of paper at once. Try to tear enough paper to completely finish a project.

If you are applying several layers of strips, it is wise to use a different color or type of paper for each layer. You can alternate between white and colored newspaper or paper toweling, using white facial tissue for the final cover.

Setting up a work area. Before starting any project, choose a work area that can easily be cleaned up. A table covered with a sheet of plastic, oilcloth, or waxed paper makes a good work surface, or you can use a plastic laminate table or counter. You'll need a container for your glue or paste (see directions for making paste on page 9), a wide paint brush or a small sponge for glue application, torn paper strips, the base or armature to be covered, and another sponge or rag for clean-up.

Choosing a base. You can apply papier mâché strips over almost any type of material, but for ease in handling, the base should be lightweight. You can use a rigid base of existing materials such as plastic bottles, tin cans, styrene, vegetables, or fruit; or, to make a special shape, use a flexible material such as chicken wire, foil paper, crushed newspaper, or clay.

The base can be removable (balloons, crumpled newspaper, foil, cardboard cylinders), or it can be integrated into the total piece for added strength. If you wish to remove the mold when the papier mâché is dry, you can apply a separator—a layer of petroleum jelly, waxed paper, or a sheet of wet paper—to keep the papier mâché from sticking to the mold.

Applying the paper strips. Using a brush or sponge, apply paste to a paper strip, press the strip firmly to the base, smooth out any wrinkles, and wipe off excess paste. The next strip should be placed so that it slightly overlaps the first. To strengthen the project, apply each layer of strips in a different direction. You can also substitute a layer of torn bed sheeting for one paper layer for added strength. Caution: Be sure to moisten each paper strip thoroughly, but do not saturate.

Balloons as a Base

Balloons are ideal bases for creating round or oval objects such as Petunia Pig (shown at right), puppet heads, or Easter eggs. Long, slender balloons make perfect dachshund bodies, while small, plump ones can be used for lightweight Christmas tree decorations. Start by selecting the size and shape of balloon you wish, blow it up, and tie the end tightly with a string. Leave about a foot of string on the end so that the project can be hung up to dry. (Use a good quality balloon and be careful not to blow it up too far or it may pop before the project is done.) Before beginning your project, coat the entire balloon surface with petroleum jelly or other lubricating cream so you can easily remove it when the papier mâché is dry. If you leave the balloon inside, it will pull away from the sides as it gradually deflates, causing a rattling sound when the project is picked up or moved around.

APPLY PAPER STRIPS *dipped in liquid starch to balloon coated with layer of petroleum jelly.*

Petunia Pig

This colorful and cheery figure is not only fun to make but is a good beginning project to help develop your skill at applying paper strips.

Making the body. Cover the balloon surface with at least five layers of paper towel strips dipped in liquid starch (see the directions for application on page 11). Alternate the color of each layer to help keep track of the number of layers. When the final layer is in place, use the string to hang the project where air can circulate freely. When the surface is completely dry, deflate or pop the balloon and remove.

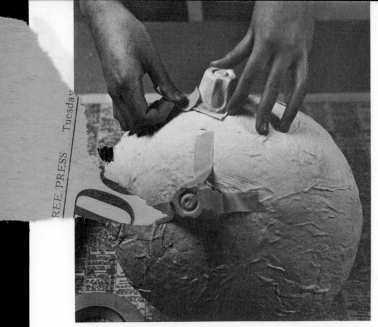

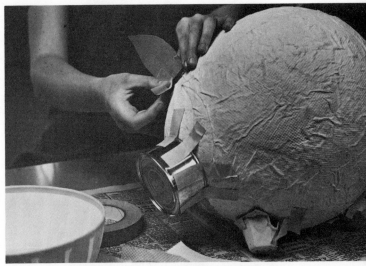

TAPE SECTIONS of an egg carton to dry surface for legs; cover with two layers of glued paper strips.

ATTACH CARDBOARD EARS with tape; for nose, use tin can (as shown here) or section of mailing tube.

Adding legs, nose, ears, and tail. Cut out egg carton pieces and tape them in place for Petunia's legs. For her nose, attach a tuna fish can or mailing tube; tape on cardboard triangles for ears. Crush a long piece of foil paper, then wind it around a pencil to shape Petunia's squiggly tail. Tape or glue in place. Then cover these pieces with two layers of paper strips dipped in flour-and-water paste. For a smooth decorating base, cover the entire figure with a final layer of white paper toweling. Allow to dry.

Finishing touches. An orange acrylic (see page 76) was used to paint Petunia's body; the flowers are red and pink (you may prefer another color scheme). Black felt pieces were glued in place for flower centers, eyes, mouth, and nostrils; yarn was used to outline her features and flower petals. Her ears were backed with fringed felt.

PEARL S. KISHIMOTO

APPLYING STRIPS TO A BASE

FRAN BREZNER

A Tiffany Lamp

A balloon blown up to a large size is used as a base to make the shade for this "Tiffany-style" lamp. Start by taping a sheet of waxed paper to the top half of the balloon. Then cover the waxed paper with three layers of glued tissue paper strips, fashioning the bottom edge into a scalloped shape. When the surface is dry, remove the balloon and the waxed paper separator, and decorate with paints of your choice. To make the base, tape a paper towel cylinder or mailing tube to the bottom of a cottage cheese carton. Cover with two layers of newspaper strips; paint when dry. For a stronger and heavier base, stuff the carton with crumpled newspaper. Using a dark yarn and white glue, outline the shade and base. Glue the center of the shade on the base.

A Japanese Dahruma Doll

A plaster-weighted base keeps this round-shaped Japanese *dahruma* doll in an upright position. To make the doll, first coat a balloon with petroleum jelly. Then apply five layers of newspaper strips dipped in flour-and-water paste. Allow to dry thoroughly; deflate and remove the balloon. Cover the open end with three layers of newspaper strips and a final layer of plaster of Paris (see page 75). Prop the doll up to dry, with the plaster base on top. To frame the face, tape rolled newspaper in place (see sketch). Then cover this ridge with paper strips dipped in paste. For the nose, tape on a rounded piece of cardboard and cover with three layers of paper strips. When dry, paint with poster paints. Coat with lacquer for a high gloss finish.

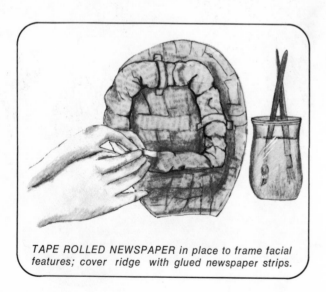

TAPE ROLLED NEWSPAPER in place to frame facial features; cover ridge with glued newspaper strips.

BARBARA HOLMAN

A Clown Puppet

This happy, round-headed puppet can be made using a small balloon. Apply two layers of glued paper strips to a balloon coated with petroleum jelly. When dry, build up facial features using paper mash (see page 66). Then cover the entire surface with three additional paper strip layers, using newspaper for the first and third layers, paper toweling for the second. Set aside to dry; then pop and remove the balloon. Use a craft knife or scissors to make this opening big enough to insert a toilet tissue cylinder for the neck. Cover the neck with two paper strip layers and the entire piece with one final layer of paper toweling. Allow to dry. Paint with a white acrylic or oil paint and coat with a clear plastic spray. Then use acrylics to paint on eyes, ears, nose, mouth, and cheeks. Glue on yarn hair and a terrycloth body. Cut out pieces of felt for hands and sew or glue in place. Add a ruff of yarn.

A Clown Head

An ideal decoration for a child's room, this smiling clown head is quickly made by covering a balloon with five layers of glued paper strips. Allow to dry thoroughly; pop and remove balloon. For the clown's ears, cut out a circle about ¼ the size of the head from cardboard or heavy paper. Cut in two, fold back the center edges about ¼ inch, and tape these tabs flat against the head; cover with two layers of paper strips. Cut out holes for the eyes. For a nose, cut out a third hole and insert a bicycle handlebar grip, a paper cylinder, or a small lightbulb. Apply paper strips over the nose, using long, narrow strips to cover the joint and keep the nose firmly in place. Use a white or light-colored paint to cover the entire head; add black and red paint for the nose, eyes, and mouth. Glue yarn in place for hair.

SANCHEZ SCHOOL, FIRST GRADE CLASS

A Popeyed Donkey

This popeyed donkey can be used as a wall decoration or a party mask. Cover the top half of a balloon with five layers of glued paper strips; let dry thoroughly. Then cut out long, tapered cardboard ears, tape in place, and cover with two layers of paper strips. For the nose, attach a cottage cheese carton, rounding the edges with mash (see page 66). Two large buttons or bottle caps can be used for eyes; tape in place and cover with mash. Or, you can cut out "eye holes" if using as a mask. When the surface is dry, remove the balloon and paint the donkey.

A Self-portrait

A snapshot of yourself will help you to make a self-portrait in papier mâché. Blow up a balloon, tie the end tightly, and tape this end to a tin can (about 1-lb. size) with the top and bottom removed. Cover with five layers of glued paper strips, using paper towel strips for the final layer. Then build up facial features with paper mash (see page 66). Set aside to dry; remove the balloon. For hair, glue on construction paper strips. You can curl the strips by pulling them across the sharp edge of a pair of scissors. Paint on eyes, eyebrows, and mouth. For eyelashes, attach fringed felt or construction paper with white glue.

CAROLINE MELANDEZ, JOAN TANTICADO, MARCELLO LAGLEVA

An Owl Bank

This owl-shaped bank with a separate base is strong enough to hold a great number of nickels and dimes. Coat a balloon with petroleum jelly and cover with three layers of newspaper strips dipped in liquid starch. To make ears and a beak, cut out three cardboard circles, make a slit to the center of each, overlap the cut edges, and secure with glue. Then make several slits around the bottom edge of each to form tabs for attaching. Glue in place and cover with three layers of newspaper strips. When the entire surface is partially dry, pop or deflate the balloon and remove. Cut feet from heavy cardboard. Then cut a strip of cardboard and tape the ends together to form a cylinder base for the body to fit over (see sketch). Tape the cylinder to the feet; then build up the feet with paper mash. When the owl is completely dry, coat with a polymer emulsion to make a hard surface for decorating. Use a knife to cut the money slot, and then paint the owl with acrylics. To highlight the eyes, glue on string circles. Then fit the decorated body over the base.

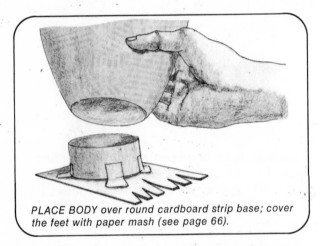

PLACE BODY over round cardboard strip base; cover the feet with paper mash (see page 66).

WILLIAM J. SHELLEY

MARLENE RUSSO

An Indian Jug

It looks like pottery, but this jug actually weighs little more than the balloon used as its base. The neck is a cardboard cylinder or strip of heavy paper taped onto the tied end of a balloon coated with petroleum jelly. Cover the neck and balloon with three layers of glued paper strips. While the jug is still partially wet, pop and remove the balloon and carefully press the bottom of the jug against a smooth surface until it sits perfectly flat. Leave it in this position until dry. For the pottery effect, paint the background a muted brown and the Indian design black.

Newspaper or Foil as a Base

Crumpled newspaper and foil make excellent bases for making papier mâché objects because they can be molded into many shapes. Foil is easier to work with because it holds the desired shape by itself. Crumpled newspaper must be secured with tape, string, or wire. Both string and tape were used to make the project shown below.

Pinocchio Puppet

You can make an entire cast of characters for a puppet play in just a few hours using cardboard cylinders, newspaper wads, paper towel strips, and liquid starch.

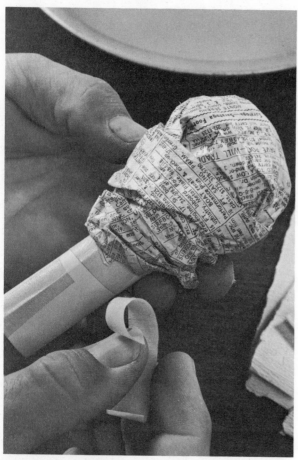

CRUMPLE NEWSPAPER around one end of cardboard cylinder for puppet head; secure with tape.

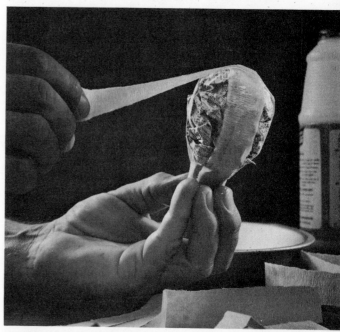

COVER HEAD with glued paper towel strips, placing each strip in an opposite direction.

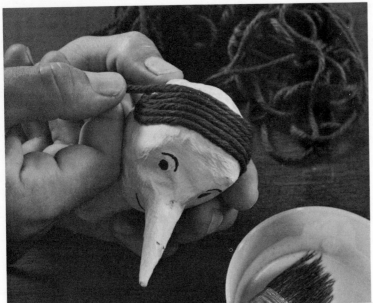

GLUE YARN to puppet head for hair after painting the entire surface with skin-colored poster paint.

Making the head. Crumple a ball of newspaper about the size of a small fist around the top of a toilet tissue cylinder or other rolled paper; secure with tape. Cover with two layers of paper towel strips dipped in liquid starch. For the nose, roll a piece of paper into a funnel about 2 to 3 inches long and tape in place. Then cover the head and nose with three layers of paper towel strips. For ears, cut out tiny cardboard circles; glue in place. Allow to dry thoroughly.

Making the clothing. Using a pattern of your choice, cut and sew a piece of bright cotton material to make the puppet's costume. For hands, glue or sew felt pieces to the sleeve ends. Tape the costume to the neck and stitch or glue a strip of felt in place for a collar. To make the cone-shaped hat, cut out a felt circle, make a slit to the center, overlap the edges, and secure with glue.

Use poster paints to make pink cheeks, black eyes, and a red mouth. Glue on yarn for hair.

A Push Me–Pull You Horse

A quick project for a beginner, this colorful horse has two heads facing in opposite directions. Cut lightweight wire into four 12-inch lengths. Then wrap a sheet of newspaper around each wire securing the edges with tape. Bend two of the wires into inverted V's for legs. To make the long necks, heads, and body, take the last two wires and bend one end of each up, the other down. Tape these covered wires together with heads facing in opposite directions. Then place the leg wires over the body just below the neck. Cover the horse with five layers of paper towel strips dipped in liquid starch. When dry, paint with poster paints and use felt pieces for the fringed mane, spots, hooves, and eyes.

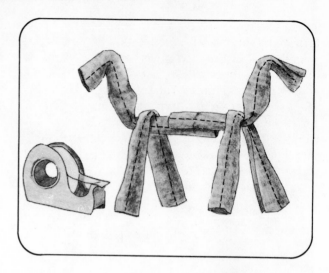

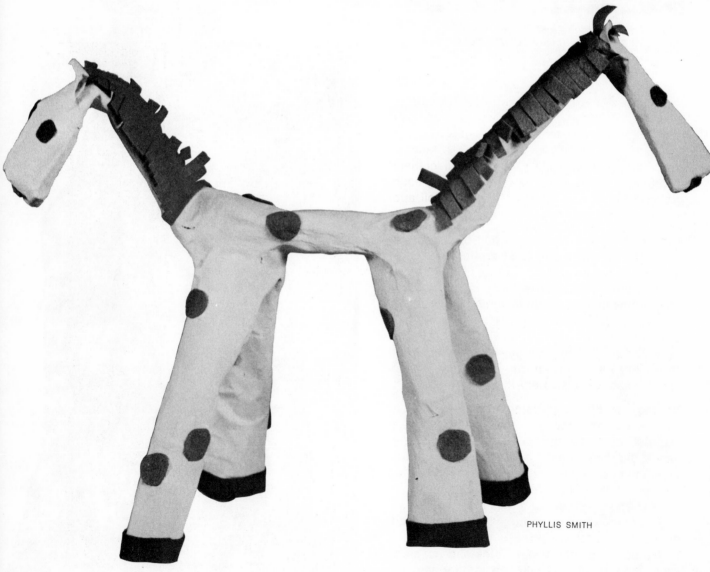

PHYLLIS SMITH

Bluebird of Happiness

Brush strokes in a blue and orange feathery pattern make this bluebird seem almost real. Make a small ball of crushed newspaper for the head and a larger one for the body. Fasten together with string and tape. Tape or glue cardboard pieces in place for wings and a tail. Insert a broken crayon or rolled paper into the head for a beak; secure with tape. Cover the bird with five layers of newspaper strips dipped in wheat paste or liquid starch. When the surface is dry, coat with gesso for a light decorating surface and paint.

STAN HUANG

A Freeform Sculpture

Crushed foil shaped into various angles and curves was used to make this freeform sculpture. To create a similarly-styled piece, simply crush heavy-duty aluminum foil into lengths ranging from 6 inches to 1½ feet. Bend these lengths into whatever shapes you wish and connect them by pressing the ends together, reinforcing each joint with additional pieces of crushed foil and ten layers of paper towel strips dipped in flour-and-water paste. Cover the entire piece with five layers of paper towel strips. Allow to dry. If desired, paint with colors of your choice.

LEE BEIGEL

REINFORCE JOINTS with a few strips of foil, then apply ten layers of glued paper towel strips.

Daisy-speckled Kitty

Spotted with daisies, this papier mâché kitten makes a good decoration for a child's bedroom. On a piece of cardboard, draw an outline of a kitten sitting with her tail to one side. Cut out this figure and tie crumpled newspaper to the back and tail for fullness. Tape two strips of cardboard to the front for legs. Build up the face with folded cardboard or crushed newspaper and attach toothpicks or pipe cleaners for whiskers. Then cover the kitten with five layers of newspaper strips dipped in wheat paste and set aside to dry. Decorate with paints, then brush on an acrylic polymer gloss emulsion for shine.

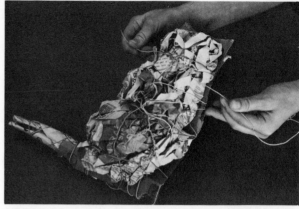

USE WIRE or string to secure crumpled newspaper to back of cardboard pattern for body fullness.

Build up face and cardboard legs by taping strips of folded cardboard in place

BONNIE LUSARDI

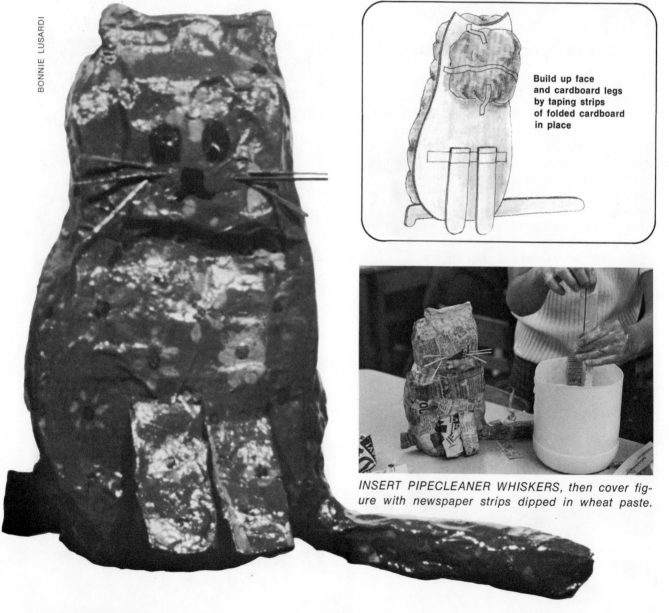

INSERT PIPECLEANER WHISKERS, then cover figure with newspaper strips dipped in wheat paste.

The Mad Hatter

Making a bust of papier mâché provides excellent experience for beginning sculptors. Mistakes can be covered easily, or the project can be taken apart and started again. To make the Mad Hatter, bend a piece of cardboard into a cylinder shape and secure the ends with tape (you can also use a large tin can for a base). Build up the sides and back of the head with crumpled newspaper taped to the cylinder. For a hat, crumple newspaper into a ball and attach to the cylinder top edge. Make a brim by cutting a hole in a cardboard circle large enough to fit over the hat. Build up facial features with shaped cardboard or crushed newspaper. Then cover the bust with five layers of newspaper strips dipped in wheat paste. When the surface is dry, paint with colors of your choice.

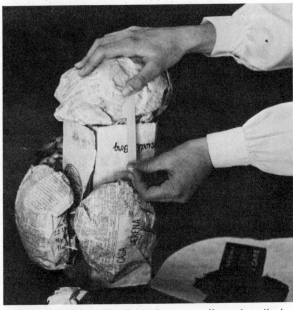

TAPE NEWSPAPER BALLS to cardboard cylinder base to form head and build up sides of face.

SMOOTH OUT WRINKLES after applying five layers of newspaper strips dipped in wheat paste.

PLACE CARDBOARD RING over crumpled newspaper head to form hat brim; secure with tape.

MARIANNE HARRIS

A Bracelet & a Mobile

Colorful and easy-to-make papier mâché bracelets, napkin rings, or mobiles make handy gifts. To make a bracelet or mobile part, fold the length or width of a newspaper sheet into a 1-inch-wide strip. Bend the strip into a circle and use tape to secure the ends. Cover with four layers of newspaper strips dipped in flour-and-water paste and a fifth layer of paper towel strips. For decoration, add a final layer of variously colored tissue paper strips, or paint in different colors. Dry thoroughly, then cover with shellac.

WILLIAM J. SHELLEY

FOLD NEWSPAPER into 1-inch-wide strips; bend strips into circles, secure ends with tape, and cover with glued newspaper strips.

CYNTHIA CLARK

HELEN COTA

Frederica Fish

This sea creature almost seems to be moving, an illusion created by the careful shaping of the body and placement of the tail. Crumple newspaper into a long, rectangular shape and secure with string. For a tail, tape on a cardboard triangle. Then cover with four layers of newspaper strips and a final layer of paper towel strips dipped in flour-and-water paste. When dry, paint with tempera and coat with shellac.

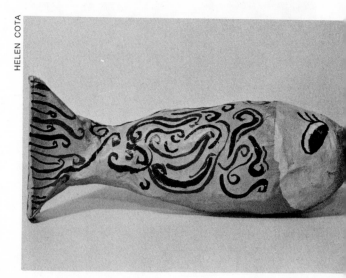

APPLYING STRIPS TO A BASE   **24**

Elephant with the Blues

By bending the trunk forward rather than down, you can make this little fellow appear to be happy instead of sad. Make the head and body by crumpling newspaper into two cube shapes, one twice as large as the other; tape together. For legs, tape on toilet tissue cylinders or heavy rolled paper. Use rolled newspaper for the trunk and rolled foil for the tail and tusks. Cut out two cardboard circles for ears and attach to the head with tape or glue. Cover the elephant with four layers of glued newspaper strips. For a smooth decorating base, add a fifth layer of paper towel strips. When the surface is completely dry, paint with tempera or acrylics. Add a coat of shellac if you want a shiny finish.

STEVE DOW

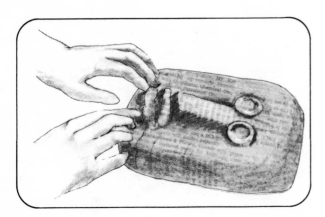

ROBERT ESCOBAR

Pink & Purple Mask

Made over an aluminum foil pan, this mask is a perfect size for wearing or hanging on the wall. Turn the pan upside down and coat it with petroleum jelly. Then apply two layers of pasted newspaper strips. For features, glue on pieces of cardboard and bottle caps and cover with three layers of paper strips. To make a smooth surface for decorating, add a final layer of paper towel strips and allow to dry. Then paint with tempera and glue on strips of construction paper and fabric for accent. Cover the mask with clear plastic spray and remove from the foil pan.

Emily, the Friendly Brontosaurus

This fanciful creature can be used as a toy for a child, a party decoration, or a prop in a puppet performance.

Making the body and head. Crumple two sheets of newspaper or foil into a ball for the body, turning the edges in toward the center. Tie string around the ball to keep it in the desired shape. Make a smaller ball for the head, flattening it into a 1-inch-thick circle. For the mouth, cut out a cardboard circle slightly larger than the head and fold it in half. With the creased edge about in the center of the head, glue the bottom half to the head. Then tape small wads of newspaper in place for eyes. For fangs, tape or glue cardboard triangles along the edges of the mouth. Attach the head to the body at a tilted angle.

Adding a tail and legs. Roll a sheet of newspaper diagonally to make a long tail; attach to the body with tape. For legs, attach two more newspaper rolls. Bend the tip of each roll for feet.

Applying paper strips. First, cover the joints (where legs, tail, and head are attached) with three layers of newspaper strips dipped in flour-and-water paste; then cover the entire figure with four more layers of newspaper strips. To make a smooth surface for decorating, apply a final layer of paper toweling strips.

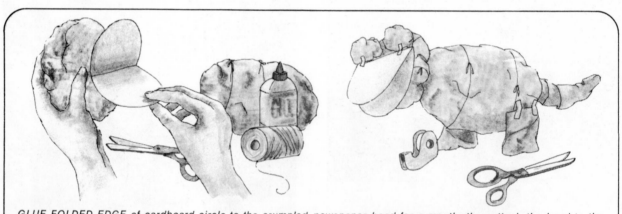

GLUE FOLDED EDGE of cardboard circle to the crumpled newspaper head for a mouth; then attach the head to the body at a tilted angle. For legs and tail, attach newspaper rolls with tape, then bend into shape.

Finishing touches. Blue and white acrylics were used to decorate this project, but you may use any color combination. To emphasize the eyes, mouth, and fangs, use contrasting colors. Cover the entire figure with a coat of clear varnish.

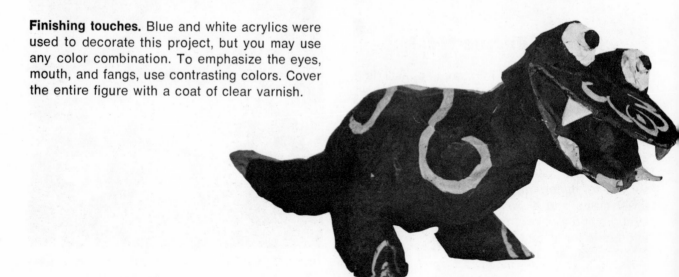

Santa & His Friends

Loosely crumpled newspaper was used as a base for making these lightweight Christmas decorations. For each one, gently crumple a sheet of newspaper into the desired shape and secure with tape or string. Use lightweight cardboard to make such features as ears, beaks, or feet. For hanging, loop a length of twine or string through a central point of the figure and knot the loose ends. Then cover the entire figure with one or two layers of newspaper or paper towel strips dipped in flour-and-water paste and set aside to dry. For a smooth decorating surface cover with gesso. Paint with brightly colored acrylics.

FOR HANGING LOOP, bend hat while still wet.

SUSPEND DUCK with twine looped through body.

ARMS, LEGS are rolled newspaper taped in place.

UNICORN'S HORN is newspaper shaped into a cone.

APPLYING STRIPS TO A BASE

Cardboard as a Base

Cardboard boxes, strips, or cut up pieces of various sizes and weights can be taped or glued together into a basic form for each project in this section. This form is then rounded and shaped with folded cardboard strips or crushed newspaper and covered with layers of glued newspaper strips. To make some of the projects very sturdy, use laminated paper strips (see page 56).

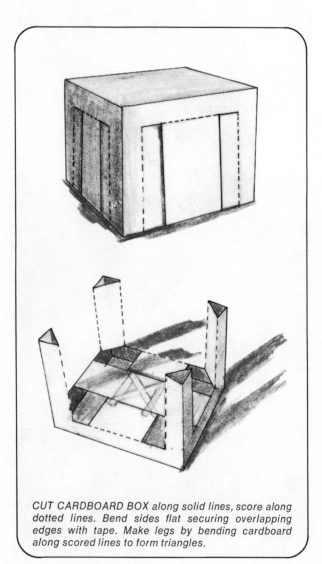

CUT CARDBOARD BOX *along solid lines, score along dotted lines. Bend sides flat securing overlapping edges with tape. Make legs by bending cardboard along scored lines to form triangles.*

Tea for Four

Large cardboard boxes and three-gallon-sized ice cream cartons were used to make this children's dinette set. Using the same method, you could build a useful coffee or end table.

Making the table. Select a cardboard box approximately 2 feet high. Following the pattern shown in the sketch at left, draw solid and dotted lines on each side of the box. Then cut along the solid lines and bend the scored flaps toward the box center until they are flat; secure with tape. Being careful not to cut completely through the cardboard, score along the dotted lines. Bend the scored cardboard into four hollow triangles securing the edges with tape.

Making the chairs and stools. To make the backed chair, simply tape a flat, rectangular box to one side of a square box turned upside down (see sketch next page). To reinforce the chair, measure from point A to B, and then from B to C, and cut a piece of cardboard this size. Bend the cardboard at point B into an L-shaped piece, and tape to the back and seat. Then cut two cardboard strips to fit into the bottom of the chair diagonally (see sketch next page). Make a slit to the center of each and insert one into the other forming an X. Tape securely in place. Reinforce the carton stools in the same way.

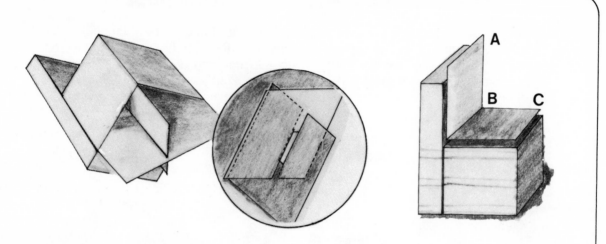

REINFORCE CHAIR by inserting two cardboard pieces which have been slit to the center and fitted together to form an X. Measuring from point A to B and then from B to C, cut out cardboard to fit. Bend at point B; tape in place.

Applying paper strips. Cover the table, chairs, and stools with six layers of newspaper strips dipped in flour-and-water paste.

For added strength, substitute laminated paper strips for regular newspaper. Spread flour-and-water paste between four sheets of newspaper, and tear into wide strips. Apply four layers of the laminated strips as you would regular newspaper strips, alternating color and direction.

Finishing touches. When thoroughly dry, coat the table and chairs with a clear varnish, or paint with tempera and then varnish. (Never use shellac on a table top or tray since it tends to water spot.)

APPLYING STRIPS TO A BASE

Decorated Coat Hangers & "Hang-ups"

You can dress up ordinary wire and wooden coat hangers by attaching cardboard boxes and pieces in various designs. The decorated hangers can also be used as lively "hang-ups" for parties or to add color to a bare wall. Cover the assembled design with three layers of newspaper strips dipped in liquid starch or flour-and-water paste. When the surface is dry, paint with bright acrylics.

TAPE CARDBOARD CIRCLES to cardboard frame. Cover "hang up" with pasted newspaper strips.

CUT CARDBOARD in shape of dog house and tape to coat hanger. Cover with glued paper strips.

COVER CARDBOARD PATTERN with glued paper strips; when dry, paint and apply coat of shellac.

GLUE CARDBOARD SHAPE to plastic hanger; cover with pasted newspaper strips, then decorate.

Bust of Napoleon

This highly stylized bust of Napoleon has a silver finish to simulate metal casting, but can be painted in natural colors. For the chest and head cut out two elongated, egg-shaped cardboard pieces. On the larger piece mark the center, score two parallel lines 1 inch to each side, fold the ends down, and fit over a cardboard cylinder; secure the edges with tape. Fold the smaller piece in half and secure two cardboard triangles between the ends (see sketch); tape to the chest. Then cut out two equally sized cardboard pieces for the hat and fit over the head. For epaulets, attach strips of corrugated cardboard to the rounded edges of cardboard pieces, taping the ends to the shoulder (see sketch).

Tape the bust to a wooden base and cover with three layers of newspaper strips dipped in wheat paste. Build up the face and chest with crushed newspaper. Use paper mash (see page 66) to make facial features. Then cover the entire bust with two layers of paper towel strips. Allow to dry thoroughly; coat with shellac. If desired, paint with white tempera, add a second coat of shellac, and highlight with silver spray.

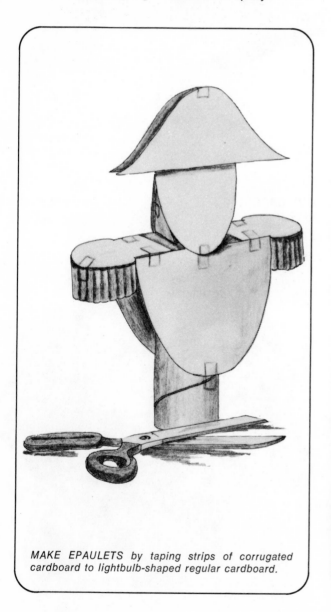

MAKE EPAULETS by taping strips of corrugated cardboard to lightbulb-shaped regular cardboard.

DENNIS MORAN

APPLYING STRIPS TO A BASE

A Prehistoric Animal

This hulking beast is an amusing and educational project for young natural history enthusiasts. Make the body and legs by taping or gluing four gallon-size ice cream cartons to the bottom of a large box. Round out the body with crumpled newspaper held in place with tape or string. For a head, shape crumpled newspaper into a large roll attaching flaps of corrugated cardboard for his lower jaw and protective neck frill. Roll sheets of newspapers into four cylinders for a long tail and three horns. Then cover the entire figure with five layers of newspaper strips dipped in wheat paste. For a smooth painting surface, add a final layer of paper towel strips. Let dry and paint with tempera.

HERBERT HOOVER SCHOOL,
FIRST GRADE CLASS

Piggly-Wiggly

This little pig's rounded body is made with cardboard half circles and strips. First cut a cardboard circle in half; then cut out a 4-inch-wide cardboard strip the length of the half circle's curved edge. Join the two halves by taping the cardboard strip between the curved edges. Cut another cardboard strip to join the bottom edges. For legs, cut four toilet tissue cylinders into 2-inch lengths and tape in place. Stuff newspaper into three of the cylinder cut ends for ears and a nose. Cover the pig with four layers of newspaper strips dipped in wheat paste; while still wet insert a twisted pipecleaner in place for a tail. When the surface is dry, paint with colors of your choice. For shine, coat with plastic spray.

KAREN FINK

Life-size Figures

These life-size figures can lend a note of color to a bare wall or empty corner. Using a large sheet of cardboard, outline the shape of a friend's body. Cut out this base and build up body fullness on one side with pieces of cardboard and crushed newspaper secured with tape and string. Cover with several layers of wide newspaper strips dipped in wheat paste. Allow to dry thoroughly before painting with tempera or acrylics.

TOM HEINRICHS, JERRY SHANNAHAN, RICHARD SLATER, WAYNE SARGENT

PAUL MASSARO, ALLEN COX

APPLYING STRIPS TO A BASE

A Box Sculpture

Using a corrugated cardboard box as a base, you can sculpt a variety of interesting papier mâché faces or portraits. Begin by selecting a square box about the size of your head. To make the features of this funny face, glue pieces of cardboard to the bottom of the box for the eyes, eyebrow ridge, bulbous nose, curvy mouth, and ears. Then cover the face with three layers of paper towel strips dipped in liquid starch. Allow to dry thoroughly. Cover with gesso to make a smooth base for decorating and paint with acrylics or tempera.

ROBERT LINDEMANN

Box Animals

These four angularly-shaped animals were made using small boxes and lids of various sizes taped together. Each figure was covered with three layers of paper towel strips dipped in flour-and-water paste. To produce a wrinkled skin effect, the elephant bank (second from left) was covered with an additional layer of un-smoothed tissue paper strips. The texture of the two figures at right was achieved by adding a layer of paper mash (see page 66). When dry, the animals were painted with acrylics and tempera and coated with a clear plastic spray.

Halloween or Party Mask

Strips of cardboard stapled together make up the base for this lightweight party mask. Once assembled to the shape you desire, cover with three layers of tissue paper strips dipped in liquid starch. When the surface is dry, apply a coat of shellac or clear plastic spray.

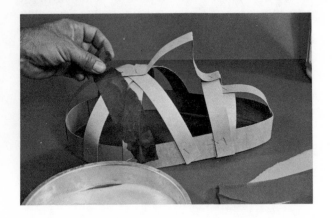

A Camel & an Elephant

A good rainy day project for children of all ages, this papier mâché camel and his elephant friend can be made large or small depending on the size cardboard boxes you have on hand. If you use small boxes, tape on toilet tissue cylinders or rolled construction paper for legs; for large boxes, use rolled strips of plain or corrugated cardboard. Shape the camel's head, neck, and humps with crumpled newspaper and attach with strong tape. Make the elephant head and trunk by crushing newspaper around one end of a paper towel cylinder or roll of heavy paper; use cardboard pieces for ears. Cover both animals with three layers of paper towel strips dipped in liquid starch. Set aside to dry, then paint with poster paints, adding a coat of shellac or varnish for shine. Glue on button or yarn eyes. Also use yarn for the camel's saddle and reins.

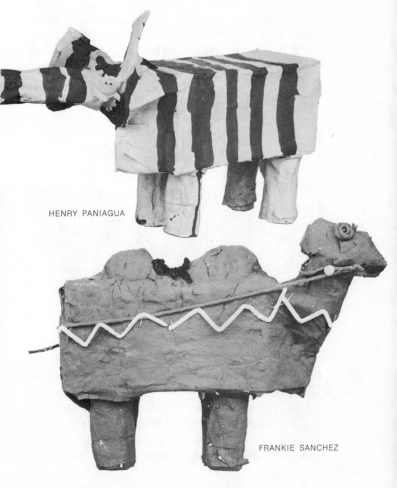

HENRY PANIAGUA

FRANKIE SANCHEZ

APPLYING STRIPS TO A BASE

CYNTHIA CLARK

Flower-topped Box

Originally a cigar box, this attractive container is strong enough to hold a multitude of small items. Carefully cut off the cigar box lid and cover both sides with three layers of paper towel strips dipped in flour and water paste; then cover the bottom portion of the box inside and out. When dry, paint with tempera or enamel. If you use tempera, apply a coat of shellac for shine. Allow to dry thoroughly before attaching yarn decoration with white glue. Secure the lid to the box with small metal hinges or strips of leather attached in place with epoxy glue.

Horse Display Case

The hollow body of this large papier mâché horse makes a delightful display case for classroom or home use. Make each leg by taping round ice cream cartons (half-gallon size) end to end. For the body, select a long box with square ends. Cut out a window at each end; then cut along the dotted lines (see sketch). Form a triangle by taping together the cut ends. For the head and neck, stuff two paper bags with newspapers, tape together, and attach to the body. Then, tape

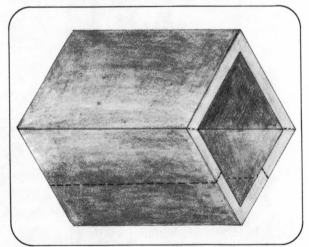

on ears made from small pieces of cardboard. Cover the horse with five layers of newspaper strips dipped in flour–and–water paste. Allow to dry thoroughly. Paint with bright tempera colors, adding a final coat of shellac for shine. Glue clear plastic wrap over both open ends of the body.

JEFFERSON ELEMENTARY SCHOOL, FOURTH GRADE CLASS

Daisy Letter Holder

Decorated with bright flowers, this papier mâché letter holder could also be used to hold napkins. Cut a piece of cardboard or heavy paper about 5 inches wide and 14 inches long. Mark the center of the length and score two parallel lines one inch to either side. Along these lines bend both ends to an upright position. Cover with four layers of newspaper strips and one layer of paper towel strips dipped in liquid starch. To make raised flowers, use paper mash (see page 66). Then cover the whole piece with two layers of tissue paper strips dipped in liquid starch, and set aside to dry. Cover the flowers with different color tissue paper, and coat with lacquer.

MARTHA SATTERTHWAITE

A Friendly Lion

The body and legs of this lion are made using a rectangularly-shaped box with windows cut out of each side. Round out the body and build up the legs by taping crumpled newspaper to the box bottom and corners. For the head, make a large ball of crushed newspaper, shaping eyebrow ridges and a nose; tape to one end of the box. To the other end, attach a tail of twisted newspaper. Tape on cardboard ears, then cover the entire figure with three layers of newspaper

ROSALYN BLOOM

strips dipped in flour-and-water paste. Allow to dry thoroughly, and paint with a tawny yellow acrylic or tempera. Make a curly mane by drawing strips of construction paper across a pair of scissors; attach with glue. Then use yarn to make a tassel for the tip of his tail and to outline his mouth. Glue on curled pipecleaners for whiskers and button or shell pieces for eyes.

Cylindrically Shaped Objects as a Base

A mailing tube, tin can, jar, bottle, paper cup, or any other cylindrically shaped object can be used as a base for making various types of papier mâché containers, lamp bases, toys, and other pieces.

Glass bottles offer great variety in size and shape; however, they are easily broken. Plastic bottles (although they lack variety) are much more durable and can be cut down for mugs or coasters, or in sections for bracelets. Turned on their sides, they can be used for making toy banks.

A Two-piece Canister Set

Tin cans of different sizes can be used to make decorative canister sets for use at home or as a gift. The two-piece set shown here was made with 1-pound and 2-pound coffee cans.

Applying paper strips. Cover both cans with three layers of paper towel strips dipped in flour-and-water paste. When the surface is dry, paint with enamel. Glue on contrasting yarn labels.

MAKE LID by tracing around canister on cardboard; cut out circle ¼ inch smaller in diameter.

FORM FLANGE by taping strip of cardboard (¾ inch wide) completely around the edge of the lid.

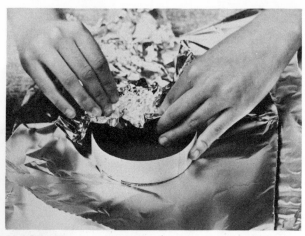

PLACE LID on two sheets of foil; crush top sheet to fit around flange and inside of lid.

ROLL AND CRUSH the bottom foil sheet into a flat brim ½ inch wide; cover lid with paper strips.

Making the lids. Place the finished canister upside-down on a piece of sturdy cardboard, trace around it, and cut out a circle ¼ inch smaller all the way around. Then cut a strip of softer cardboard about ¾ inch wide and long enough to wrap around the circumference of the circle. Tape the strip to the cardboard circle, forming a flange (see photo on page 38). Place this cardboard base, flange side up, on two sheets of foil paper. Crumple the top sheet and press it firmly over the flange and onto the inside of the lid. Roll the edges of the bottom sheet up to within ½ inch of the flange and press the roll flat to form a brim. Cover with three layers of paper towel strips.

To make a knob for the lid, push a nail up through the foil-covered circle. Wrap the point with several thicknesses of foil paper and cover with three layers of paper towel strips. Allow to dry, and then paint the lid. Glue yarn around the knob to match the canister labels.

BARBARA HOLMAN

Daisy-trimmed Napkin Rings

Daisy-shaped fabric trim (available at m____
age or variety stores) was used to deco____
perfectly rounded napkin rings. To ____
holders, cut toilet tissue cylinders into 1____
lengths. Cover each piece (inside and out, ____
careful to cover the edges) with six lay____
newspaper strips dipped in liquid starc____
⅛-inch layer of paper mash (see page 66____
to dry thoroughly, smooth the edges ____
sandpaper, and paint with tempera. C____
plastic spray. Cut out fabric designs and glue
in place. As an added finishing touch, glue felt
strips to the inside of each holder.

RAY GARCIA

A Toy Soldier

Straight-backed and square-shouldered, this toy
soldier makes a lively birthday party centerpiece
or a decoration for a boy's room. Tape two cardboard strips to the bottom of a square-topped
bottle for feet. Fold newspaper into strips for
arms. For a head, tape a styrene ball or a crushed
newspaper ball to the bottle neck. Cover the
figure with three layers of paper towel strips
dipped in flour-and-water paste. When thoroughly dry, paint with tempera or acrylics and
coat with a clear polymer emulsion gel.

CAROL ISHIKAWA

Mother & Child

Similar in design to Mexican pottery, this figure of Madonna and Child can be made using a small salad oil or wine bottle. Cover the bottle with three evenly applied layers of narrow newspaper strips dipped in liquid starch. To make the child, fold newspaper into a 1-inch-wide strip and tape it to the bottle at an angle. Cover with five layers of newspaper strips. When the surface is dry, paint on expressive faces and a design of your choice.

Three-part Pencil Holder

This pencil holder has separate compartments made by taping three toilet tissue cylinders together. For the bottom, place the unit on a piece of cardboard, trace around it, cut out, and tape in place. Cover the outside of the holder with three layers of newspaper strips dipped in liquid starch; add a fourth layer of paper towel strips. When the surface is dry, paint with poster paints. Then coat with a clear acrylic emulsion gel for shine. Edge the holder at top and bottom with glued-on yarn.

ESTHER HORNIK

Siamese Twins

These two inquisitive feline companions were made with light bulbs taped to the tops of wine bottles (large soft drink bottles would work equally well). The tails are lengths of wire wrapped tightly with newspaper strips dipped in liquid starch and taped in place. Cardboard triangles were used for ears. The twins were covered with three layers of newspaper strips plus a final layer of paper towel strips for smoothness. After the figures had dried, tempera paints in delicate pastels were used to decorate.

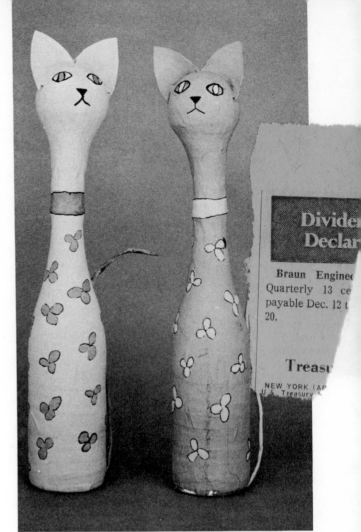

PAM TYLER

CINDY WIGNAL

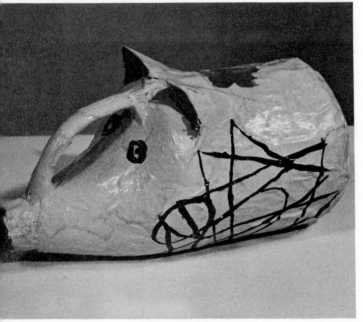

A Wistful Pig

Woebegone and listless, this little stray pig is a good candidate for finding a home with other members of a beloved animal collection. The base for making the pig is a plastic bottle (with handle) turned on its side. Tape cardboard triangles in place for ears. If desired, add legs made from egg carton sections or rolled strips of cardboard. Cover the pig with three layers of newspaper strips dipped in flour-and-water paste. When dry, paint with poster paints and add shellac for shine.

Milk-bottle King

An empty milk bottle and crushed newspaper make up the base for this brooding, majestic figure. Shape his head and beard with loosely crumpled newspaper tied or taped around the bottle neck. For a crown, tape on cardboard triangles. Then cover the entire piece with two layers of newspaper strips dipped in liquid starch. Use paper mash (see page 66) to build up facial features. Cover with three layers of newspaper strips. When the surface is dry, paint with tempera or poster paints. If desired, cover with shellac for shine.

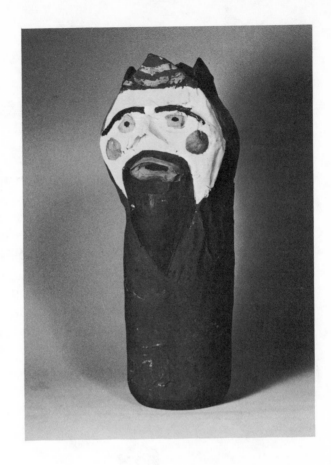

LAURA LEE GREENE

Tin Can Alley Cat

Sitting ramrod straight and alert, this beribboned cat is made with two coffee cans taped together end to end and topped with a paper bag. For the head, stuff the paper bag with crumpled newspaper, turn it upside down over the top coffee can, and secure with tape. Make cone-shaped ears by cutting out two cardboard circles, slitting each to the center, and gluing the overlapped cut edges and taping in place. For the bow, use cardboard rectangles glued or taped together. Cover the cat with three layers of newspaper strips dipped in wheat paste. Insert toothpick whiskers while still wet. When completely dry, paint with black and white paints. Coat with a clear plastic spray for shine.

Wire as a Base

Both single strand (or spool wire) and sheet wire (hardware, chicken, or window screen wire) can be easily manipulated into a base for making unusual papier mâché figures.

Sheet wire is most often used for building very large pieces because it is sturdy and holds its shape. To work with this wire and the thicker spool wires, you'll need a pair of pliers and a wire cutter or tin snips. To protect your hands, fold masking tape over the sharp edges, or wear gloves. Single strand wire (although not as sturdy as sheet wire) is popular for making smaller pieces because it can be molded into intricate shapes, curves, and angles (see project below).

BEND WIRE into skeleton shape. Insert left leg wire through staple attached to wood base.

Girl with a Balloon

This lightweight and whimsical figure is made using single strand wire, foil, a fresh egg, a rectangular block of wood, and newspaper and paper towel strips and squares dipped in flour-and-water paste.

Making the body. Bend lengths of wire into a skeleton shape (see sketch at left). Make legs and arms by wrapping wire pieces to the body. Secure the left leg wire to the wooden block with a staple. Then crush foil around the wire skeleton (see photo on next page) to mold the body shape, and cover with three layers of pasted newspaper strips. Set aside to dry. For a balloon string, bend another length of wire to the end of the left hand wire and secure with narrow strips of masking or cellophane tape.

CRUSH FOIL around the wire skeleton to fill out body contours, and to make hair and clothing.

COVER EGGSHELL with three layers of glued newspaper squares; make hole for balloon "string".

Making the balloon. Using a straight pin, poke a hole in each end of a raw egg (if the egg is at room temperature it will blow out more easily); carefully blow the egg out. Cover the shell (a ping pong ball would work equally well) with three layers of small newspaper squares. When dry, use a nail to make a hole in one end and insert the tip of the balloon "string" wire. Secure with cellophane tape.

Finishing touches. For a smooth decorating surface, cover the figure and balloon with a layer of paper towel strips. When dry, paint with enamel or acrylics.

CYNTHIA CLARK

GIRAFFE, ZEBRA are made of plywood base covered with chicken wire and glued newspaper strips.

LYNDA J. EVANS

MAKE OSTRICH FEATHERS by dipping pleated paper towels in liquid starch and folding in half.

DE ANZA SCHOOL

COVER CAMEL with final layer of whole sheets of brown tissue; then coat with clear plastic spray.

Playground Sculptures

Sturdy enough for playground use, the camel is constructed with chicken wire and plywood. Using a large sheet of plywood, cut out a single piece for the head, body, and hump; then cut out four legs and four circle feet. Attach body and leg pieces to a rectangular-shaped plywood piece with angle brackets and screws (see photo at left). Also use angle brackets for attaching feet to legs. Cover the wooden frame with chicken wire, weaving cut ends together with single strand wire (drape sheets of newspaper over the frame for use as a guide in estimating the amount of wire you'll need).

To make a smoother surface for applying paper strips, cover the chicken wire with a layer of foil. Then apply three layers of newspaper strips dipped in flour-and-water paste. When dry, decorate with paints or colored tissue paper and coat with a clear plastic spray. If you expect the camel to receive hard use, bolt the feet to a slab of concrete.

The giraffe, zebra, and ostrich can be made using the same materials and construction methods as described above.

A Super Mouse

This sturdy mouse with the big round ears is 3 feet tall. Cut and shape chicken wire for a base, securing the ends with heavy tape. To strengthen the ear joints, insert chopsticks or lengths of heavy gauge wire into the head and tape to the back of the ears. For a tail, roll chicken wire into a long cylinder and attach with wire pieces. Cover the mouse with five layers of newspaper strips dipped in flour-and-water paste. To keep him from tipping over, add sand to your paste and apply three additional layers of newspaper strips to the bottom half of the body. Paint with acrylics, and coat with acrylic polymer emulsion or shellac for shine. Glue on burlap eyelashes and whiskers dipped in liquid starch.

TRUDI EDELMAN

Snake in the Grass

Viewed from a distance, this giant-sized snake could appear surprisingly real. To make it, roll chicken wire into long cylinders. Place the cylinders end to end, interweaving the wire ends with single strand wire. Bend the connected cylinders into the desired snake shape and cover with three layers of newspaper sheets dipped in flour-and-water paste or liquid starch. When dry, cover with colored tissue paper squares. Glue on a paper fang and curled eyelashes.

HOOVER ELEMENTARY SCHOOL

A Sailor Man

Supported by an intricately-shaped wire armature, this well-known figure should be made only after you have tried your skill making other wire bases. You'll need galvanized window screen wire, hardware wire, 1 by 2-inch wood pieces, cardboard, newspaper, a 3-gallon ice cream carton, commercially prepared paper mash, and wheat paste. The figure is made in duplicate halves which are wired together, then covered with glued newspaper strips.

Making the head and neck. Using corrugated cardboard, cut out two head and neck silhouettes. Attach crumpled newspaper to both pieces of cardboard with masking tape to fill out the shape; then cover with a ¼-inch layer of paper mash (see page 66). When each surface is thoroughly dry, smooth with sandpaper, then remove the crumpled newspaper and cardboard base.

Making the body. Form rounded shoulders by pressing window screen wire (cut into a 16-inch circle) into a 3-gallon ice cream carton (see photo). Placing both hands in the middle of the wire circle, press the wire down into the carton until it becomes a dome-like shape, then remove. Next, wrap a sheet of hardware wire around the carton, weaving the cut edges together with single strand wire.

Remove the ice cream carton and drape the dome-shaped wire over one end of the wire cylinder (see photo); secure with single strand wire. To make the bottom ridge of the cylinder, bend a narrow strip of galvanized window screen wire into a half circle and fit around the cylinder. Secure the ends with single strand wire. Using tin snips, cut out a key hole and slots in the cylinder (see photo) for the windup key. Then cover the cylinder with a ¼-inch layer of paper mash, leaving a 1-inch space along the vertical center. When the paper mash is dry, cut the cylinder into two halves along the uncovered space. Bend the exposed wire back to form tabs.

Making the arms and legs. Using a felt marker or grease crayon, draw two short arms (with hands), two birdcages, and four leg halves on a sheet of hardware wire. Cut out the parts with tin snips, wearing gloves to protect your hands. Bend the cut edges down to give a rounded contour. Also bend the wire to form fingers and ridges on birdcage (see photo at right). Then attach each arm to a birdcage half with single

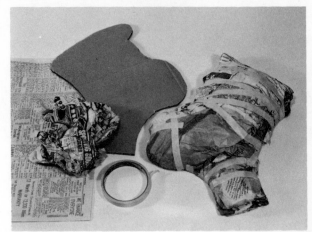

CUT OUT CARDBOARD SILHOUETTES for head, neck; tape on newspaper to build up contours.

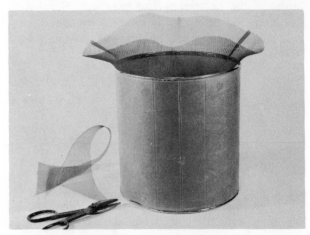

FORM DOME-SHAPED SHOULDERS by slowly pressing sheet of wire into ice cream carton or cylinder.

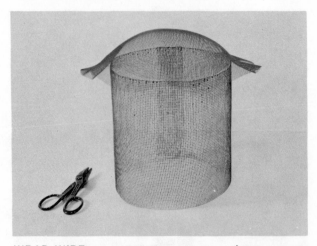

WRAP WIRE around carton, secure edges, remove carton. Attach shoulders with wire lengths.

WILLIAM J. SHELLEY

CUT WIRE CYLINDER (covered with paper mash) into two halves, cut out key hole and slots for arms.

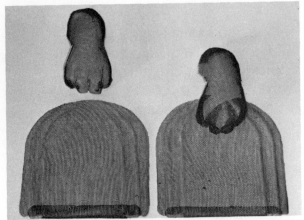

BEND WIRE to form fingers, birdcage ridges; attach hands to birdcages with single strand wire.

APPLY PAPER MASH to leg, arm, and birdcage shapes, using a knife or tongue depressor.

ATTACH BODY HALVES to wooden armature made of 9-inch cross bars and a 12-inch vertical bar.

strand wire. Coat each leg and arm-birdcage unit with a ¼-inch layer of paper mash. Allow to dry thoroughly. Then wire together two leg halves to form each leg.

Assembling the parts. Cut out a half circle from the top of each shoulder dome to make room for the head and neck piece (see photo); glue each half in place. Wire the arm and birdcage units to the outside of the body cylinder halves at the slot marks. Then make a wooden armature from three 1 by 2-inch strips of wood to hold all parts together. Nail two 9-inch-long cross members to the inside of each side of the body from the outside, then attach a 12-inch-long vertical piece to the cross members. Nail the bottom of one neck half to the top of the upright piece. So that the legs will swing freely, attach the top of each leg to the armature with a bolt and nut. Drill a hole in the middle of the upright piece for inserting the windup key.

Finishing the sculpture. Cover each assembled body half with three layers of newspaper strips dipped in wheat paste. Set aside to dry. Then wire the two body halves together at 6-inch intervals. Glue on cardboard tabs along this seam to simulate the metal tabs seen on many metal toys. Coat the entire figure with two layers of shellac, allow to dry, then add two coats of white acrylic paint. When the surface is dry, use bright acrylics to paint on clothes and other decorations. Then bend a ⅜-inch steel bar into a key shape and insert into the key slot.

Other Objects as a Base

You can use almost anything as a base for making papier mâché pieces—from lightbulbs, old hats, fruit, or vegetables to pieces of styrene, plastic, or glass. Whatever the object, it should have the basic shape you need or one that comes close to it (you can always use some of the materials discussed in earlier sections to change or add onto the shape for the desired effect).

Maracas or Noisemakers

By using an orange as a base, you can make a Mexican maraca or a baby rattle. You will also need two ½-inch dowels and a package of dried, edible beans.

Applying paper strips. First, cover the orange with petroleum jelly for easy removal later on. Then apply six layers of paper towel strips dipped in flour-and-water paste. Be careful not to use too much paste, or the surface will not dry rapidly enough and the orange may spoil. For a smooth surface, add a final layer of paper towel strips.

APPLY six layers of glued paper towel strips to orange which has been coated with petroleum jelly.

CUT DRY SHELL in half with knife or sharp scissors; remove orange base, tape halves together.

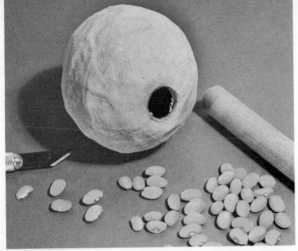

CUT HOLE in dry shell and drop in enough beans to make rattling sound; then insert the handle.

Place on waxed paper and allow to dry for at least 48 hours, turning the covered orange two or three times during this period to permit even drying. Then draw a line around the center for a cutting guide. Using a sharp knife, cut the dried papier mâché into two halves and remove the orange. Tape the two halves together and cover the joint with two layers of paper towel squares. Then cover the entire surface with a layer of paper towel strips. Allow to dry.

Adding the handle. Using a craft knife, cut a hole ½ inch in diameter in the maraca. Drop in several beans to make the rattling sound. Put a drop of white glue on the end of a ½-inch dowel; then push the dowel into the hole until it touches the other side. To hold it in place, drive a nail through the surface into the top of the dowel.

Finishing touches. To strengthen the maraca, coat it with shellac. When it is dry, use acrylics to paint on a Mexican design. Remember to use non-toxic paints for a baby's rattle.

WILLIAM J. SHELLEY

APPLYING STRIPS TO A BASE

Funny-paper Bowl

Eye-catching and sturdy, this serving bowl featuring comic strip characters would be ideal to use at a teen-age party or outdoor gathering. For a base, choose a bowl with a wide opening, turn it upside-down, and coat the outside with two layers of paper strips soaked in water. Then apply five layers of newspaper strips dipped in flour-and-water paste, keeping the bottom edge even. For a final layer use strips of newspaper comics. When the paste has dried, remove the papier mâché bowl from the base and coat the inside and outside surfaces with shellac.

WILLIAM J. SHELLEY

Vegetables & Fruits

These lightweight papier mâché fruits and vegetables are easily and quickly made for displaying in a bowl. Simply coat a real vegetable with petroleum jelly (for easy removal later), then cover it with five layers of newspaper strips dipped in flour-and-water paste. Allow to dry, then cut the surface in half and remove the base. Tape the two halves together, covering the seam with newspaper strips. Glue on paper stems where needed and cover the whole piece with a layer of paper towel strips. When dry, coat with shellac, then cover with a white acrylic paint. Add a coat of tempera and polymer gloss medium for a high shine clear finish.

WILLIAM J. SHELLEY

A Court Jester

Quickly made using a lightbulb and a paper cup, this court jester will lend a note of humor to a party table setting. Place the neck of the light-bulb in a large paper cup and secure with tape. Cover the bulb and cup with three layers of newspaper strips dipped in liquid starch. When the surface is dry, build up the nose, ears, pointed head, and boutonniere with paper mash (see page 66). Then apply two additional layers of newspaper strips over the entire surface. Set aside to dry. Paint the jester with bright acrylics or tempera and add a shiny coat of shellac.

MARIE BECAAS

A Mexican Hat

You can use a styrene hat from a pizza parlor, an old hat, or a party hat from a variety store as a base to make this colorful Mexican sombrero. Begin by attaching a wide circle of heavy cardboard to the brim with rubber cement and tape. Then crumple newspaper and tape to the hat top for a rounder and fuller shape (see sketch). Drape a large sheet of newspaper over the built-up crown and secure with string or a rubber band. Cover the hat (inside and out) with five layers of newspaper strips dipped in liquid starch. Add a final layer of paper towel strips. Set aside to dry. Paint with bright red acrylics, adding yellow trim; for a shiny surface cover with a coat of shellac. Glue on balled fringe and a ribbon hatband.

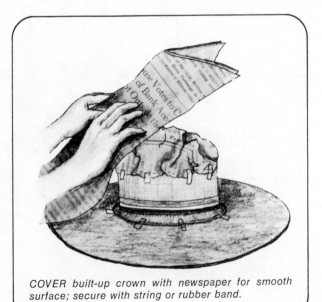

COVER built-up crown with newspaper for smooth surface; secure with string or rubber band.

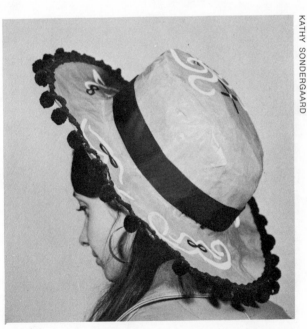

KATHY SONDERGAARD

COVER STYRENE BALL with two layers of paper strips soaked in wheat paste, overlapping the edges.

COAT DRY SURFACE with gesso or white paint to make a smooth surface for painting and decorating.

INSERT WIRE ENDS of hanging loop into decorated ornament after threading through cord or string loop.

Christmas Ornaments

Styrene balls (readily available in different sizes at most variety stores) can be used as a base for making unusual and brightly colored Christmas ornaments. Begin by covering a ball with two layers of wheat paste-soaked newspaper strips. When dry, apply a coat of gesso to make a smooth decorating surface. Then paint with brightly colored acrylics and add a coat of polymer emulsion for shine. For decoration, glue on ribbon strips, sequins, yarn, buttons, shells, or other small objects. To make a hanging loop, thread a short piece of lightweight wire through a cord or string loop. Twist the wire ends together and push them into the styrene ball, leaving only the cord loop showing.

SUKI GRAEF

A String Puppet

This string puppet is made using a paper cup for the head and a paper towel cylinder for the body. Tape one end of the cylinder to the bottom of the cup and cover both with three layers of paper towel strips dipped in wheat paste. After the surface has dried, paint on facial features. Using scraps of material, cut and sew a costume and hat; glue in place. Make the pompom hat tassel, buttons, and ears by wrapping yarn around a piece of cardboard, removing the cardboard, tying the yarn at one end, and cutting the loops at the other end. Then cut out cardboard hands and feet and loosely tie or sew in place. To manipulate the puppet, loop thread or lightweight string through his hands, feet, and other parts of the body as desired; attach these strings to a block of wood or heavy piece of cardboard.

The Red Baron

Toothpicks and matchsticks are glued together with white glue to form the lightweight frame of this model airplane. Make sides, top and bottom of frame, and wings separately on a piece of waxed paper, then glue the sections together. For wheels, glue on cardboard circles. Soak an ice cream stick in hot water for about 15 minutes, then twist into shape for a propeller; attach with a straight pin or nail. Then dip small pieces of white typing paper in white glue thinned with water (½ water, ½ glue) and attach to the wing, frame, tail, engine, and sides of cockpit with full strength white glue. When dry, the typing paper will become taut and smooth. Attach strings for struts and glue on a cardboard Red Baron.

55

Working with Laminated Paper

Laminated sheets or strips of paper can be used to make papier mâché pieces where a greater durability is required or desired. A quick and easy process, lamination consists of spreading paste between sheets of paper (usually four or more). (Although many of the projects in this chapter call for using newspaper to make laminations, any type of paper you have on hand will work equally as well.) When the paper becomes limp and pliable, you can tear it into strips or leave it as a whole unit before applying to a base. You can also cut out a specific pattern or shape and bend or mold it into a final form without any base supports. If you want to make a piece very strong (such as a piece of furniture), substitute a layer of bed sheeting for a layer of paper.

Choosing the paste. You can use any of the adhesives discussed on page 9 to make laminations. Wheat paste is strong but is not as easy to make as the others. Diluted white glue is also quite strong, however when used in large quantities, it can prove to be expensive. For smaller objects, it works very well with bond paper or paper towels.

Applying the paste. Begin by mixing the paste in an aluminum foil pan or other disposable container. Then use a 3 to 5-inch paint brush to spread the paste between the sheets of paper. Do not apply any of the paste to the outside surfaces of the layered paper or it will become too sticky to handle. Allow the paste to set for a few minutes until the paper becomes pliable. Then tear it into strips or shape or mold the entire sheet as you wish. The paper will be quite stiff and hard when dry.

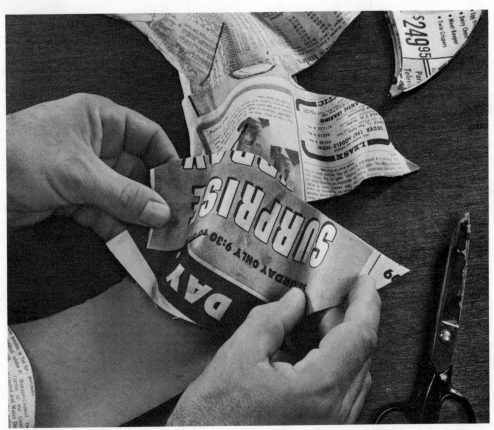

Laminated petals are used to make sunburst frame (see page 63).

A Leaping Frog

Set and ready for a giant-sized leap, this sturdy freeform frog will be a continual delight in the imaginative playtime fantasies of any child. To make it, first crumple newspaper into three flat-domed balls (see photo below). Then laminate four sheets of newspaper with wheat paste and while still wet, cut out the basic outline of a frog. Drape the laminated paper over the flattened paper balls, fold and slit the paper to form the desired shape, and temporarily secure with stick pins. For the eyes, glue on small rolls of newspaper. Then cover the entire outside surface of the frog, overlapping the edges, with a layer of newspaper strips dipped in wheat paste. When the surface is completely dry, remove the crumpled paper base and coat the frog with shellac. Apply a prime coat of white acrylic paint, decorate and add a final coat of shellac for shine. The papier mâché fish and dove shown on the opposite page are made the same way.

USE STICK PINS to keep laminated pattern in place as you shape and mold it over newspaper base.

COVER BASE with layer of glued newspaper strips; allow to dry thoroughly and coat with shellac.

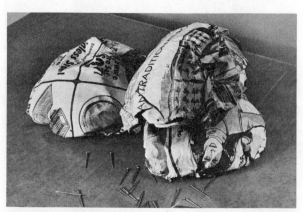

CRUMPLE NEWSPAPER into three dome-shaped balls for a base; secure shapes with tape or string.

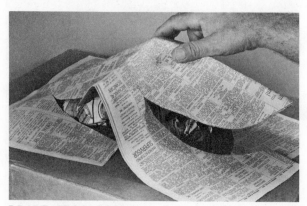

DRAPE FROG PATTERN of laminated paper over crumpled newspaper base while the paper is still wet.

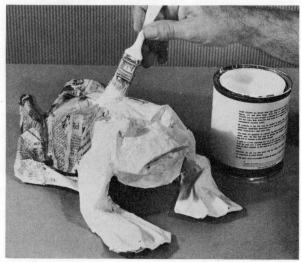

APPLY GESSO (after removing newspaper base) to make a smooth decorating base; then paint.

WORKING WITH LAMINATED PAPER

WILLIAM J. SHELLEY

A Dove & a Fish

DOVE BASE is crumpled newspaper; cover with damp laminated paper pattern and mold into shape.

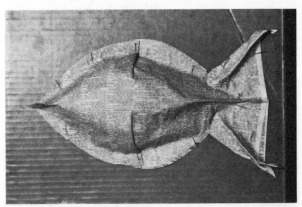

FOLD AND PIN laminated paper into desired fish shape after draping it over newspaper base.

COAT WITH SHELLAC to seal; when dry, paint with white acrylics for a subtle, muted effect.

SEAL FISH with coat of shellac; set aside to dry thoroughly. Then paint with colored acrylics.

A Jungle Table

Originally this project was intended to be a simple table, but the laminated paper legs buckled during the drying process. Some imaginative thinking turned this bad luck into an unusual jungle table. The wrinkled legs were reminiscent of elephant legs, so a little paint was added for toes and a "leopard" table top.

To make each table leg, laminate four newspaper sheets with wheat paste and roll into a cylinder; secure the edges with glue. The table top is constructed like a tray. Laminate several sheets of newspaper and fold up each side about four inches. Miter the corners as shown in the photograph at right and fasten with paper clips. Then smooth the tray edges with newspaper strips (see photo at right). For a tablecloth effect, remove the paper clips while the paper is still damp and shape the corners as desired. When the legs and tray top are dry, attach the legs to the top with glue and strips of newspaper. Paint and coat with a clear plastic spray.

MITER CORNERS of table top; secure with paper clips to keep the folds in place.

COVER EDGES with newspaper strips dipped in wheat paste; when dry, attach table top to legs.

USE WIDE BRUSH to apply wheat paste between newspaper sheets; roll into cylinders for legs.

FORM TABLE TOP by folding each side of partially wet laminated paper into 4-inch widths.

WILLIAM J. SHELLEY

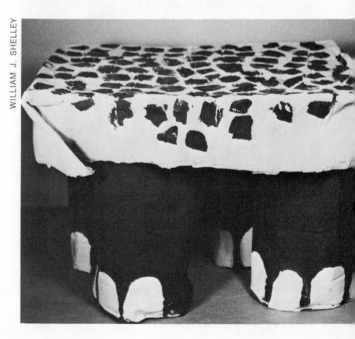

Comic-strip Wastebasket

This durable and unusual wastebasket is a laminated paper cylinder. Begin by spreading wheat paste between five sheets of newspaper, using the comic section for the bottom or top layer. When the laminated paper is pliable, roll it into a cylinder with the comics on the outside. Use paper clips to hold the loose edges in place while you smooth out any wrinkles. Then apply paste to the overlapping edges and stand the cylinder on end to dry. If the paper cylinder starts to sag during the drying process, use your hands to smooth out the wrinkles. To make the wastebasket bottom, place the cylinder on a piece of cardboard and trace around one end. Cut out the circle and attach in place with tape or several strips of newspaper comics dipped in paste. Cover the bottom and top edge with three layers of paper strips. When dry, brush on two coats of clear shellac.

USE NEWSPAPER STRIPS *dipped in paste to attach and cover cardboard bottom and reinforce edges.*

APPLY PASTE *to overlapped edges of laminated paper, then shape into smooth cylinder.*

USE PAPER CLIPS *to keep laminated cylinder in shape while it dries; smooth out any wrinkles.*

WILLIAM J. SHELLEY

A Striped Tiger

Unlike his real-life brother, this shy creature only seeks a loving and protective home. First laminate four sheets of newspaper with flour-and-water paste. Then draw a pattern (see sketch at right). Cut along the dotted lines and roll the body, head, legs, and tail into cylinders, securing the shapes with pins and string. For ears, cut out laminated paper triangles, slit at the base and overlap the edges to form rounded cones; attach to the head with newspaper strips dipped in flour-and-water paste. Cut out four laminated paper circles for feet, making slits in several places to form tabs and attach with newspaper strips. Allow to dry thoroughly, then paint with acrylics.

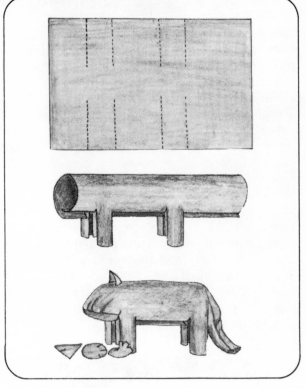

An Op Art Chair

Durable and attractive, this tiny tot's chair is made with a 3-gallon ice cream carton and two pieces of cardboard. To add strength to the chair seat, cut out a cardboard circle and tape to the closed end of the ice cream carton. Then cut out a rectangular piece of cardboard for the curved back and tape it to the seat edge. Cover the entire chair with four layers of laminated paper strips and a final layer of paper towel strips dipped in flour-and-water paste. Let dry thoroughly. Use black and white tempera or poster paint for the checkered design.

WORKING WITH LAMINATED PAPER

Spray Can Cover

You can dress up your bathroom with colorful containers for hair spray and other toiletries. First, cut two sheets of newspaper the exact height of the can or bottle and long enough to wrap around it. To prevent the final laminated cover from sticking to the can, wrap one of the newspaper sheets around the can, leaving a ¼-inch space between the paper and can. Use a sponge to dampen the second sheet, wrap it around the dry sheet, and secure the edges with tape. Then laminate four sheets of newspaper with liquid starch and wrap around the dampened paper base. Overlap edges and secure with glue or tape. Allow to dry.

For the lid, cut out a cardboard circle slightly larger than the diameter of the container and a ½-inch-wide cardboard strip about ½ inch longer than the circumference of the circle. Tape the strip around the circle edge to form a rim. To make the curled lid decoration, bend tightly rolled newspaper or foil into shape, secure with tape, and glue to the lid. Cover the lid and decoration with three layers of newspaper strips. When the container is dry, paint and decorate.

CYNTHIA CLARK

Sunburst Mirror

Fringed with petals, this sunburst mirror can decorate a bathroom or dressing area. To make the mirror base, cut out two corrugated cardboard discs 2½ inches wider than the diameter of the mirror. Cut a hole in each disc—one the actual size of the mirror and the other ½ inch smaller than the mirror. Then laminate four sheets of newspaper with liquid starch. While the paper is still damp and pliable, cut out enough petals to frame the wider cardboard disc. Slit the flat end of each petal, and overlap the slit edges to form conical humps. Then curl the petal tips. When the petals are dry, place them around the wider cardboard disc and secure with glue. Glue the remaining cardboard to the back of the petaled disc. Paint the petaled frame with a bright color and glue decorative yarn around the inside circumference. Then glue the mirror to the frame back.

WILLIAM J. SHELLEY

Flower Pins or Candle Holders

These brightly-painted flowers can be used as ornamental pins or decorative candle holders. Your choice of petal shape and color is almost unlimited (two patterns are shown below). To make a flower, draw and cut out a flower pattern three times on the damp top surface of laminated bond paper four layers thick. Curl the petals around a pencil or shape them with your hands. If you are making a candle holder, leave sufficient room in the flower center to hold a candle. Insert the three laminated patterns one inside the other, gluing them together at the centers. Dry the flower in the oven (175°) with the door open, then paint with bright acrylics. For use as a pin, glue a ready-made clasp (available at variety stores) to the flower back. Add paper mash to the center of the candle holder to assure perfect fit.

ADELINE AND FRED BAGUIO

Rice Papier Mâché

A simulated rice paper wall hanging, screen insert, or window pane covering can be created with laminated sheets of paper. Begin by securing a piece of waxed paper (slightly larger than you want your finished piece to be) to your working surface. Then arrange leaves, ferns, tissue paper shapes, or dried flower blossoms on the waxed paper in a design that pleases you. When the pattern is completed, remove the pieces, coat the waxed paper with liquid starch, and quickly replace each part. Using a sponge and a patting motion, apply additional starch over the entire surface. Pull apart facial tissue sheets; then place single sheets over the design, patting gently so no bubbles remain. Allow to dry for 48 hours, then coat the front with a protective plastic spray.

ELINOR PARSONS

PLACE DESIGN ELEMENTS on waxed paper which has been coated with liquid starch.

LIGHTLY PRESS sheets of facial tissue over design; smooth out any bubbles, wrinkles.

Making and Using Paper Mash

Paper mash is a claylike material made from bits of paper that have been soaked in paste (see discussion on kinds and making procedures on page 9). The paste slowly breaks down the paper fiber and turns it into a pulpy, malleable material.

Paper mash can be modeled into various shapes and forms or applied to a base in order to round out or enlarge the shape or add texture. You can leave the texture as is, or sand lightly with fine sandpaper for a smooth finish. While the paper mash is still wet, other materials (such as string, pebbles, beads, or buttons) can be pressed into the surface as decoration.

How to make paper mash. You can buy commercially prepared paper mash at most hobby or variety stores, but if you plan to work in this medium with any frequency, it's a good idea to make your own. You can use any one of the following procedures:

By soaking toilet or facial tissue in liquid starch you can make a smooth and extremely pliable material. Saturate the tissue and then squeeze out the liquid. The more liquid you squeeze out, the faster the mixture will become a firmer consistency. If you do not plan on immediately using the paper mash, cover it with liquid starch and store in the refrigerator.

Another way to make paper mash is to cover pieces of an egg carton with liquid starch, paste you have prepared, or any commercial glue. Soak the paper for six to eight hours, then squeeze out the liquid until it becomes a good consistency for modeling. For added strength, a different texture, or a wood-like surface, add sawdust to the mixture.

Paper mash may also be made by soaking small, torn pieces of newspaper (1/4 to 1-inch squares) in liquid starch, paste, or glue. (Two sheets of newspaper will provide enough malleable material for making most of the projects shown in this chapter.) Let the paper soak for 48 hours, then squeeze out the liquid until it becomes the desired consistency. To make a finer consistency of paper mash using this technique, soak the newspaper pieces a second time in warm water. Squeeze out the water until you have a firm pulp; then add enough starch, paste, or glue to make the paper mash workable.

To make paper mash which has an extremely smooth consistency, pour a cup of water into a blender, add one cup of paper mash using any one of the mixing procedures described above and mix until thoroughly blended. Strain the paper mash through a colander to remove excess water.

A Bowl of Fruit

By covering bases of crumpled newspaper, you can create realistic-looking pieces of fruit. Start by crumpling newspaper into various fruit shapes; secure with string or tape. Using a knife, cover the base with a ¼-inch layer of commercial paper mash. Place the fruit in a 175° oven with the door open until thoroughly dry. Then smooth any rough places with sandpaper, apply a coat of gesso to provide a smooth decorating surface, and paint with acrylics. Using an ice pick or a nail, make a small hole in the top of the dry fruit and glue on cardboard stems.

COVER EACH BASE with a smooth layer of paper mash; set aside to dry thoroughly.

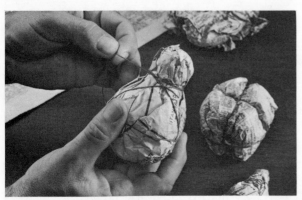

TIGHTLY CRUMPLE NEWSPAPER into various fruit shapes; secure with string or tape.

APPLY GESSO to each fruit piece to make a smooth decorating surface. Glue on paper stems.

WILLIAM J. SHELLEY

MAKING, USING PAPER MASH

Baroque Mirror Frame

The raised, elaborate design of this mirror frame was created with cardboard pieces and paper mash. To make the frame, cut out a square piece of corrugated cardboard. Then cut a scalloped design on each side. In the cardboard center, cut out a circle slightly smaller than your mirror. Glue on pieces of cardboard for the raised designs. Cover the entire frame with a combination of homemade and commercial paper mash. To add swirling patterns, press string into the paper mash when it is partially dry. Allow the frame to dry thoroughly, then paint. To emphasize the design contours, cover the frame with antiquing liquid (see page 77). When the paint is dry, place the mirror in position against the frame back and secure with glue.

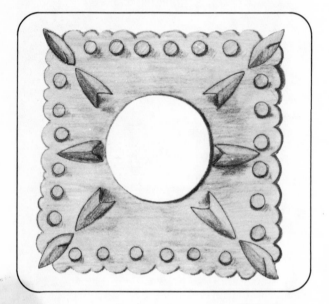

EARL HEINRICHS

North-wind Medallion

The paper mash covering of this unusual medallion was antiqued to bring out the sharp contrasts in texture. First, cut out a round wooden base (an old mirror frame could be used) and glue on pieces of corrugated cardboard to build up the basic design. Then cover the design with a thick layer of commercial paper mash, or use any of those discussed on pages 66-67. While partially wet, use a knife or clay modeling tool to carve out special details and contours. Set the medallion aside to dry. Paint with white paint, then rub in antiquing liquid (see page 77).

EARL HEINRICHS

A Classic Urn

Similar in design to the pottery of ancient Greece, this urn was built with jar lids, cardboard pieces, tin cans, and paper cups. The entire piece was then covered with paper mash. Begin by taping or gluing together two large jar lids, a paper cup, a tin can, a larger tin can, a rim made from cardboard, an inverted paper cup, a small tin can, a pointed paper cup or cone, and two cardboard strips bent into handles (see sketch). Then crumple newspaper to round out the surface. Cover the urn with a thick layer of paper mash. When the urn is partially dry, use a knife or a clay modeling tool to carve out details. For a draped design, press thin rope, string, or yarn around the center of the urn. Add a knob of paper mash at the top of the urn. Allow the urn to dry thoroughly and then paint.

EARL HEINRICHS

CHRIS POPOVICH

A Flowered Bowl

If the consistency of the paper mash is firm enough, you can model it into this daisy-covered bowl. First, make the paper mash by mixing ¼-inch squares of newspaper with slightly diluted white glue. When the paper mash is firm, but still pliable, squeeze and press it into shape for the bowl bottom. Then begin slowly building up the ¼-inch-thick rounded sides until the bowl is the desired height. Allow the bowl to dry thoroughly, then paint with acrylics and coat with polymer gloss medium for shine.

A Stone-like Head

Although it looks like stone, this carved head was made by covering a tin can and cardboard base with paper mash. Begin by turning a two-pound coffee can upside down and taping or gluing cardboard pieces and crushed newspaper in place for facial features, hair, and a beard. Then cover the entire head with a thick layer of paper mash. While the paper mash is still wet, carve out hair and other facial details, using a knife, an orange stick, or a clay modeling tool. Let the head dry thoroughly, then apply various tones of brown paint.

EARL HEINRICHS

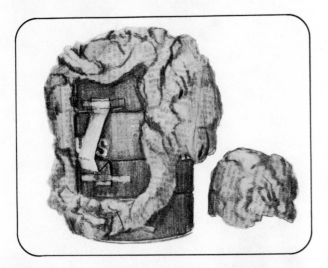

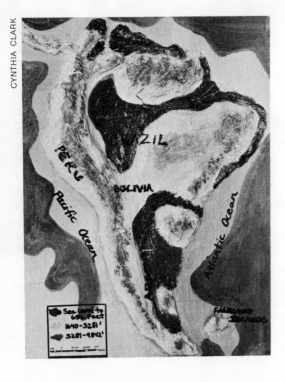

CYNTHIA CLARK

A Map of South America

You can easily create a bas relief map for classroom or home use using a plywood base and tissue paper mash. First, draw an outline of the desired area or country on the plywood sheet. Then dip sheets of facial tissue in liquid starch, squeeze them out, and press into place for mountains, ridges, or hills. Set the map aside to dry thoroughly, then paint as desired. Include a color key in the corner to indicate different altitudes.

Clown with a Daisy

The grainy texture of this speechless-appearing clown is produced with commercial paper mash. The figure itself is made using a wine bottle, a balloon, and a piece of wire. Place a cork in the wine bottle, and tie a blown up balloon to the cork. Then cover the entire piece (except for the bottom of the wine bottle) with a layer of commercial paper mash. For a collar, cut out a strip of cardboard, 1 inch wide and 5 inches long, and tape it to the paper mash-covered bottle neck; cover with paper mash. While the surface is still partially wet, insert short pieces of copper wire for arms. Bend the wire into shape and cover with paper mash. Also use the paper mash to build up ears, nose, and mouth. Then insert a plastic flower into the clown's hand and press plastic eyes in place. Allow the figure to dry thoroughly, then paint with bright acrylics. Glue on short pieces of yarn for hair.

RALPH JOOSTEN

WILLIAM J. SHELLEY

A Jewelry Ensemble

You can make these jewelry pieces with paper mash, a ring of plastic, and laminated paper (see page 56). To make the bracelet, cut out a ring from a plastic starch bottle, shorten it to fit around your wrist, and tape the ends together to make a ring. Cover the outside surface with a thick layer of paper mash and carve out a design of your choice. Set aside to dry.

The bead necklace is made by shaping paper mash into small balls and threading them onto a knitting needle or piece of wire. When the beads are dry, decorate with paints. Then remove the beads and string them.

To make the flower pin, cut out two flower patterns from four layers of laminated paper (see page 64). Curl the petals of each over a pencil, and glue the tips to the bottom at the center; glue the two parts together. To build up the center, apply a mound of paper mash.

You can speed the drying process for all three pieces by placing them in a 175° oven with the door open for a few hours. When each piece is thoroughly dry, paint with bright acrylics, and coat bracelet with antiquing liquid (see page 77).

An Unusual Clock

Paper mash is used to make the raised flower designs on this unusual papier mâché clock frame. To make the frame, cut out the corners on a square piece of corrugated cardboard. Then score (being careful not to cut all the way through) the cardboard about 2 inches in from each side (see photo below). Bend up each side to make a shallow box and secure the corners with tape. In the box center, cut out a circle to fit the clock shape. For a snug fit, cut out a strip of cardboard, 2 inches wide and long enough to wrap around the clock perimeter and tape to back of frame (see photo at right). Then cover the face and sides of the frame with white paper strips dipped in a solution of ⅔ white glue and ⅓ water. When the frame is dry, place mounds of commercial mash onto the surface and carve out each flower design with a knife or clay modeling tool. Outline the bird forms, flowers, frame edge, and center circle with heavy string or yarn dipped in white glue. Coat the ornaments with gesso for a smooth decorating surface, then paint the flowers and frame. Insert the clock from the back.

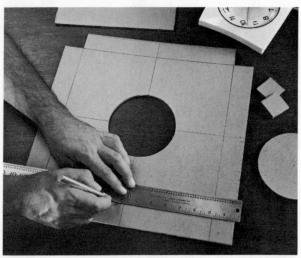

SCORE CARDBOARD along each side after cutting out the corners and a center circle.

PLACE CLOCK in housing made of cardboard strip taped to frame; clock should fit snugly.

CARVE FLOWER DESIGNS in mounds of paper mash, glue on cord to outline frame, bird shapes.

WILLIAM J. SHELLEY

MAKING, USING PAPER MASH

Finishing Papier Mâché Projects

When the construction of your papier mâché project is complete, decorating possibilities are practically endless. You can use any of a variety of paints in many colors, then add paper, yarn, or other decorative materials. Choose your color scheme and design motif to complement your piece. Often, you will be able to add color and texture with various items found in the sewing basket. For example, an old ball of yarn could be used to make a lion's mane and tassel tail, or a piece of felt could be glued in place to outline specific facial features.

PREPARING THE SURFACE

To make a smooth, light-colored surface for decorating, it is a good idea to cover a project made with newspaper with a layer of white toweling, tissue paper, bed sheeting, or a coat of gesso (see below). Without this covering, you will need several coats of paint to cover the newspaper. When the project is thoroughly dry, use fine sandpaper to smooth any rough edges before decorating.

Applying Gesso

Gesso is a white, opaque liquid with the consistency of cream. It is used with most papier mâché projects to provide an even surface for decorating. You can buy gesso in most variety or craft stores, or you can make it with materials found around the house or classroom. Acrylic gesso may be used with any type of paint, but acrylic paint can *only* be applied over acrylic gesso.

APPLY GESSO to make a smooth, light-colored surface for decorating. Allow to dry thoroughly, then use fine sandpaper to smooth any rough areas.

To make gesso, pour 1 cup of evaporated milk into a blender, add 4 sticks of white chalk (½ stick at a time), and blend until creamy. You can also combine 1 part white powdered tempera paint with 1 part evaporated milk and shake in a bottle until creamy. Store this mixture in the refrigerator.

Apply gesso with a brush and allow to dry thoroughly before painting.

Applying Plaster of Paris

Plaster of Paris can be used to add strength or texture to the surface of a papier mâché object, or to add weight to the base or bottom part of a figure for better balance. You can apply plaster directly to a piece, or for added strength and easier application, you can coat strips of cloth and apply them to your object.

You can make a good modeling plaster by mixing 2¾ pounds of dry plaster of Paris with 1 quart of water. It is a good idea to make your mixture in a plastic bowl that can be thrown away later, or use the bottom half of a plastic bleach bottle.

If a scale is not available for weighing the dry plaster, pour a pint of water in the mixing bowl and slowly sprinkle plaster into the water. Continue adding dry plaster until it forms a small mound above the surface of the water. Let the plaster soak up the water for about two minutes. Then, using your hand or a long-handled spoon, stir slowly along the bottom of the bowl to keep the whole mixture moving. Air bubbles will rise to the surface. Gently tip the bowl from time to time to cause more air bubbles to rise. Remove any scum that may form on the surface (this is a sign of old plaster; if an excessive amount forms, discard the plaster).

When the mixture is still creamy, but has enough body to adhere, it is ready to use. You can apply it directly to your piece with a knife or a small trowel, or dip a damp cloth (muslin or bed sheeting) into the mixture. Coat well and apply the plaster-coated cloth to the armature. Because plaster sets up in about 15 minutes, you must apply it to your project quickly and evenly. After the plaster is dry, it may be filed or sanded smooth, then painted.

DECORATIVE FINISHES

When the gesso or light-colored paper layer is dry, you are ready to paint and decorate. You may wish to antique your piece to bring out contrasts in texture, or you can add individual touches with yarn, beads, or paper cut-outs.

Selecting Paint

Bright, bold colors are ideal for decorating toys, masks, puppets, and holiday pieces, while other projects require a pastel. Whatever the choice of paint, you can lighten the color value by adding small amounts of white paint.

The paints most commonly used with papier mâché are tempera, poster paint, water colors, acrylics, oil paints, and enamel. Each paint has its own special quality, and you may select one for its particular effect, easy availability, or cost. In general, water-base paints are easier to apply and dry faster. Another advantage is that smudges or painting errors are easily removed. Although not as easily applied by an amateur, oil-base paints are extremely durable and are resistant to water or other dampness.

Tempera is a water-soluble, opaque, powdered paint available in shaker cans; it is used extensively in craft or art subjects throughout many school systems. To make tempera, mix 1 part liquid (either water or starch) with 1 part powdered paint; adjust the paint-liquid balance to change the thickness for producing various effects. Mixed with evaporated milk, tempera becomes waterproof. To make colors brighter, add 1 tablespoon sugar to each cup of mixed tempera.

Poster paint is a concentrated, opaque, water-soluble paint that comes in bottles. It dries to a dull surface. You can thin it by adding water.

Water colors are transparent, water-soluble paints that come in cakes (in tins or palettes) or tubes. To dilute concentrated water colors, dip your brush in water and then into the paint.

Acrylics can be either transparent or opaque water-base paints which dry to a waterproof surface. Available in tubes and bottles, acrylics can be mixed with a matte medium for a dull finish or with a glossy medium for a shiny finish. Brushes used for application can be cleaned with soap and water while they are still wet.

Oil paints require a little practice for applying an even finish. When dry, the surface will have an opaque but dull finish. You'll need paint thinner or turpentine for clean-up.

Enamel is a quick-drying, oil-base paint that comes in a high, medium, and low gloss. Available in jars or cans, enamels are usually opaque. To clean your brushes, you'll need paint thinner especially made for enamel.

Antiquing Papier Mâché

Pieces decorated with paper or water-base paints (except acrylics) may be antiqued with commercially available varnish or "instant ager" (a solution made by mixing 1 tablespoon of instant coffee powder with 1 cup of canned milk).

Using a clean cloth, rub the antiquing liquid over those surfaces you want treated. Use several applications over specific areas where you want shadows, "age", or interesting color changes. Use the liquid lightly where only subtle color changes are desired.

To achieve a more aged effect, cover the project with antiquing liquid; rub down, allow to dry, and sand the surface lightly with very fine sandpaper. You can repeat this process up to a dozen times, with each process producing a finer finish. This is especially effective on pieces decorated with paper labels.

JEANNE VALENTINE   JEANNE VALENTINE

ANTIQUED SURFACE emphasizes the contours and texture of this clown's body.   *RUB ANTIQUING LIQUID over surface to highlight edges or intricate shapes.*

You can also antique a piece by rubbing black or brown paint (diluted with either water or a solvent to a coffee tone) over the painted surface with a rag, sponge, or brush. Use the same kind of paint for antiquing as you did for painting the surface. Repeat applications to those areas you wish darkest. Rub the liquid to blend over the entire area rather than stand out in one spot.

For oil-painted surfaces, you can achieve an antique look by painting or rubbing the entire surface or small areas with varnish, thinned with turpentine. Repeat applications after each coat is dry.

Decorating with Other Materials

You can glue on labels, postage stamps, playing cards, wrapping paper, wallpaper, magazine pictures, or other cut-outs to decorate your papier mâché projects. Use white glue or rubber cement to secure these decorations in place.

Yarn, string, felt, discarded jewelry, buttons, fabric pieces, colored toothpicks, pipe cleaners, or shredded tissue paper can also be used to decorate papier mâché.

ADD FINISHING TOUCHES or outline shapes by gluing on cord, string, yarn, shredded tissue paper, fabric, buttons, or other decorative objects.

PROTECTIVE FINISHES

Papier mâché projects can be treated with any one of the chemicals or protective coverings discussed below to make them fireproof, waterproof, and more durable. It is especially advisable to fireproof papier mâché candlesticks since the surface will be exposed to flame as well as drippings of hot wax. Trays, garden sculpture, and children's toys should always be waterproofed.

Fireproofing

An easy way to make a papier mâché piece fireproof is to mix 1 teaspoon of sodium phosphate (available in most drug stores) with each cup of liquid adhesive used to apply paper strips, laminate paper, or to make paper mash.

Strengthening and Waterproofing

A coat of shellac will give a hard, protective coat to most papier mâché pieces, but is susceptible to water spots. White shellac is clear, and orange shellac leaves a slightly darker finish.

Clear plastic sprays are very effective for producing a completely waterproof finish. Hold the can at least 10 inches from the piece and spray, moving the can rapidly over the entire surface, for an even covering.

Lacquer is perhaps the most popular protective finish used for papier mâche. Besides waterproofing and making the piece more durable, lacquer gives a nicely finished look. It is clear and can be diluted with a lacquer thinner to achieve specific highlights. Lacquer is most effective if three to five coats are applied, but each coat must be thoroughly dry before the next is brushed on.

Varnish is also effective as a water repellent. If you used it to produce an antique finish, your piece is already waterproofed.

Other Projects

DAVID GILHOOLY

JEANNE VALENTINE

HANGING SLOTH has a chicken-wire base covered with foil, glued newspaper strips, paper mash.

BALLOON LIGHT FIXTURE can be made with wire or balloon base and glued newspaper strips.

JIM LA BRIOLA

CANDELABRA'S chicken-wire base is covered with plaster of Paris for added strength, weight.

OVERSIZED SINK PLUG is made with chicken wire, then covered with glued newspaper strips.

PHOTOGRAPHERS
Most of the photographs in this book were by **William J. Shelley,** including the front cover and the inside front and back covers. Exceptions are as follows: **Carol G. Blitzer:** 79 (bottom right); **Glenn Christiansen:** page 54 (top, center, bottom left); **Erwin Lang:** page 6 (bottom right); **Jack McDowell:** inside front cover (top row middle), inside back cover (top row middle); **Museum of International Folk Art** (Santa Fe, New Mexico): 6-7 (top); **Eugene Stein:** page 7 (top right); **Darrow Watt:** pages 17 (top), 18, 19 (top), 34 (bottom), 54 (right), 57, 63 (bottom), 68, 72 (bottom), 73.